Praise for *The New Japan: Debunking Seven Cultural Stereotypes*

The New Japan is definitely recommended as an insightful textbook for cultural studies for Japanese college students who now search for their own cultural identity in a drastically transforming world.... [T]he author's unique discussion for creating an individualistic collectivism for Japan's future is tremendously educational for international students as well.

—Akio Inoue
Professor and Director of Oyasato Institute for
the Study of Religion, Tenri University

David Matsumoto speaks in a unique voice in his critical analysis, The New Japan. *It is the voice of the Japanese diaspora. Matsumoto is a Japanese American who is not only a first-rate social scientist but also a major actor in the world of international judo competition. He has spent a lifetime traveling back and forth between the U.S. and Japan, living, working and playing. He is able to integrate three sets of data: the findings of a host of well-executed social psychological studies, including his own; the findings of national surveys conducted by the Japanese government and media; and his own participant observations of the land of his ancestors. The result of this integration is the articulation of a major challenge facing Japan in the twenty-first century, the harmonic creation of what Matsumoto calls "individualistic collectivism." This is a ground-break-*

ing analysis which takes us beyond the conventional dualisms of the intercultural field.

—Jacqueline Wasilenski
International Christian University, Tokyo

At a time when we Japanese have to reexamine our strengths and weaknesses during the current transitional period, The New Japan *is a timely contribution. The author (himself a Judo player and having Japanese roots) has [written] a resource book for reflective but forward-thinking Japanese and for those who have Japanese partners in their business...lives. With this book in hand, we [will] no longer suffer from stereotypic...conceptualizations of Japanese culture. I recommend this book for my friends all over the world.*

—Toshihiro Kanai, Ph.D.
Professor of Organizational Behavior
Graduate School of Business Administration,
Kobe University

THE
NEW
JAPAN

David Matsumoto may be reached at dm@sfsu.edu for further information about his research and the contents of this book.

DAVID MATSUMOTO

THE NEW JAPAN

Debunking Seven Cultural Stereotypes

First published by Intercultural Press. For information contact:

Intercultural Press, Inc.
PO Box 700
Yarmouth, Maine 04096 USA
Tel: 207-846-5168
Fax: 207-846-5181
www.interculturalpress.com

Nicholas Brealey Publishing
3-5 Spafield Street
London, EC1R 4QB, UK
Tel: +44-207-239-0360
Fax: +44-207-239-0370
www.nbrealey-books.com

© 2002 by David Matsumoto

Production and design by Patty J. Topel

Printed in the United States of America

06   05   04   03   02   1   2   3   4   5

Library of Congress Cataloging-in-Publication Data

Matsumoto, David Ricky.
    The New Japan: debunking seven cultural stereotypes / David Matsumoto
        p.   cm.
    Includes bibliographic references
    ISBN: 1-877864-93-5
        1. Japan—Civilization—1945–   I. Title.
    DS822.5.M3674 2001
    952.05—dc21   2001051919

Dedication

To Paul Ekman
Mentor, Colleague, and Friend
I am proud to call him my teacher

Table of Contents

Figures

Unless indicated otherwise, the vertical axes in all figures presented in the book represent the actual scales used and reported in the research cited. In some cases these were scales based on scores from instruments used uniquely in those studies; in others they were percentages. More detailed information concerning the exact nature of the data can be obtained by contacting David Matsumoto or by referring to the original research cited.

Tables

Acknowledgments

I am indebted to many people who have helped me along the way in the production of this book:

To my friend and colleague in Japan, Atsuo Miki, who encouraged me to write a book like this and gave me valuable guidance and suggestions along the way. Thanks for your friendship and support in not only this book but all my writing endeavors.

To Professor Kyoko Yashiro of Reitaku University, who read the entire manuscript and made many suggestions for improving the text. Thank you also for your friendship and collegiality throughout the years.

To Professors Yohtaro Takano and Susumu Yamaguchi of Tokyo University, who provided me with valuable references and helped foster my interest in cultural values in contemporary Japan. Thank you for the many opportunities you provided me and for the wonderful discussions we have had over the years on the topics discussed in this book.

To my editor at Intercultural Press, Judy Carl-

Hendrick, and all others there who worked on the text, who encouraged me to work on this project, and went well above and beyond the call of duty in editing (in such a professional way, I might add) my unintelligible writing and transforming it to semi-intelligent (I hope!) prose. I thank you for your professionalism, insight, wisdom, and encouragement.

To my wife, Mimi, for providing the best home environment within which anyone could possibly work, for reading the entire manuscript from start to finish in various forms, and for providing me with important feedback at each step of the way. Thank you for being you.

To my children—Sayaka, Satoshi, and Masashi—who really had nothing to do with this book but are three of the best kids in the world, and I just wanted to say that. Thanks.

Even though I have been lucky enough to have the help and support of these and many other people too numerous to mention here, any mistakes or problems in the book are unquestionably mine and mine alone.

—David Matsumoto
San Francisco 2002

Foreword

Kyoko Yashiro
Reitaku University

In *The New Japan* David Matsumoto presents a complex reality of Japan that many scholars of Japanese culture have failed to address in English so far. He gives convincing evidence from current studies and surveys that show that generalizations made from previous works about Japanese people and culture no longer hold with younger generations. His explanation of how this change was brought about and what kind of turmoil Japanese society is currently facing demonstrates his intimate and deep contact with Japanese people and society. His proposals for solving the problems are pertinent and welcome.

Indeed, the older generation, meaning those who grew up before WWII, were collectivistic, had interdependent self-concept and interpersonal consciousness, controlled emotion, had seemingly limitless loyalty to their company and work, and had strong marital commitment. Many Japanese still cling to these images because they believe these are their fundamental values. However, as Matsumoto argues, data from the younger generation show that Japanese are becoming as individualistic as westerners (or even more so or in different ways), and place more importance on emotions than Americans in interpersonal relationships. And with preference given to specialists rather than generalists in the business world, the younger generation is moving away from loyalty toward companies and moving toward self-satisfaction and fulfillment in their jobs. The same can be said for their concept of marriage; they marry for love, not for the family.

The older generation lament the deterioration of morality among the young, calling them shin-jinrui (new humans), and feel powerless in directing them to keep the tradition. Matsumoto's model of cultural change sheds some light on the issue. He proposes that Japan is going through rapid change from a low resource availability-population dense culture to a high resource availability-population dense culture. In this process traditional collectivism culture has changed into individualism/collectivism duality culture, but it is not changing into a complex individualistic culture like the U.S.

The sense of powerlessness currently shared by the older generation was largely created by defeat in the war and the subsequent post war education. As Matsumoto points out, the U.S. occupation force succeeded in implementing "democratic" and "individualistic" education. But we need to understand that this process stripped Japanese of their confidence in their concept of country and people on which to base their education of the young. Thus, education of the young was largely left to mothers in the homes and young new teachers in the public schools. Fathers' absence from home and community greatly contributed to decay in social morals of the young, though it brought about miraculous economic growth to Japan. Moral decay in affluent society–Japanese style is what we have now.

In Japan there is a lot of discussion on how to cope with changing society and younger generations of workers. Matsumoto outlines new management styles, new teaching materials and methods, new family relationships necessary in business, schools and homes respectively. As a judo master, he expresses his sincere hope that sports will be used to teach high moral standard as well as excellent skills. These arguments and hopes are shared by many enlightened managers, educators, and parents in Japan today. Matsumoto's *The New Japan* is a strong endorsement to those who are striving to bring about many of the practical and pertinent proposals Matsumoto puts forth in this book.

–Kyoko Yashiro
Professor, Reitaku University

1

Japanese Culture, Past and Present

Contemporary Japanese culture is considerably different from previous, traditional notions of it and from most people's current stereotypes, including those of the Japanese themselves. Japan is commonly and stereotypically known as a land of nobility and chivalry with values such as honor, pride, and perseverance. These form a moral code of everyday living that has permeated Japanese society for generations, even centuries. Yet, contemporary Japanese culture (especially for younger Japanese) seems to operate from different values, attitudes, beliefs, norms, and behaviors. In short, Japan is evolving into a society with a different culture.

In this book I will explore the nature of the cultural and social differences in contemporary Japanese culture as compared with traditional Japanese culture. Chapter 1 describes classic and then contemporary

conceptualizations of Japanese culture, demonstrat-
ing how they paint a picture of a homogeneous,
unicultural Japan that has existed for centuries. Academics and laypersons alike, as well as Japanese and
Westerners, have all painted the same picture, and
these stereotypic images and perceptions of Japan
have, for all intents and purposes, *become* Japan. Toward the end of this first chapter, I will explore current
instability in Japan. Then I will present data to support the hypothesis that there is a substantial degree
of unrest, apprehension, and dissatisfaction in the
country today, and I will suggest that these worries
exist at least partially as a result of a clash of cultural
dualities in contemporary Japan. In short, I believe that
the view of a tranquil, homogeneous Japanese culture can no longer be supported.

In chapter 2 I will present data from selected research in social psychology comparing Japanese individuals in Japan with those in other countries and
from polls and surveys conducted in Japan by Japanese companies and the Japanese government in recent years. While it is impossible to survey all possible
research related to the points I make in this chapter,
these data should give any reader reason to question
stereotypic notions of contemporary Japanese culture.
In chapter 3 I will speculate about the reasons for
Japan's dramatic cultural and social change in the past
few decades. In chapter 4 I will describe the impact of
the changing Japanese culture on everyday life in Japan. Finally, in chapter 5 I will provide some food for

thought concerning the various directions, shapes, and forms Japanese culture and society may take in the future.

Classic Conceptualizations of Japanese Culture

For over a century, Japanologists have characterized Japanese society and culture as homogeneous, centered on a few core values, personality traits, and moral virtues. These views have been promulgated by Japanese and non-Japanese alike, in academic and non-academic circles. While a comprehensive review of the literature is beyond the scope of this book, I will review below what many believe to be some of the classics in the study of Japanese culture, highlighting the considerable similarities in their portrayals of Japan.

A pivotal episode in the history of Japan that had a great influence on the study of the country and its culture is the Meiji Restoration. Prior to the Meiji Restoration in 1862, Japanese society was basically closed off from the rest of the world by the government established by the Tokugawa Shogunate. The Meiji Restoration refers to the events in Japanese history that led to the overthrow of the Tokugawa Shogunate and the restoration of governmental power by the emperor, who took the name of the Meiji (enlightenment) Emperor.[1]

With the Meiji Restoration came open trade, exchange of peoples, and the flow of ideas across borders. Consequently, interest in Japan and in the Japanese culture began to flourish. Much of this interest may have been due to Westerners' sense of wonder about Japan; it was so different from any other country with which they were acquainted. This sense of marvel led to writings in many areas of social science. Historians, for example, began to study and write about the history of Japan, and Japanese literature became available to the rest of the world; for example, Westerners were introduced to the *Tale of Genji* (*Genji Monogatari*), *The Pillow Book* (*Makura no Soshi*), and other such works. And, of course, with these works came knowledge of Japan's culture and people.

From the late 1880s until the period immediately following World War II, a number of major works became classics in our understanding of Japanese culture and its people. They not only provided penetrating and insightful analyses of Japanese culture, knowledge of which was relatively unavailable to the rest of the world for literally centuries, they also provided non-Japanese with explanations for the curious and often baffling aspects of Japanese behavior.

One of the earliest and most often cited works, for instance, about Japanese culture from an outsider's point of view was that of the English-educated, Irish-Greek writer Lafcadio Hearn. In his book *Glimpses of Unfamiliar Japan* (1894), Hearn portrayed the Japanese as a humble, persevering people who, in the face of danger, threat, grief, and other disheartening emotions, managed to maintain a sense of dignity about themselves and smile. He saw the Japanese as people who had instituted politeness as a social rule—who brought mannerisms and etiquette in social interaction to their highest standard. In the preface to his work, he wrote,

> But the rare charm of Japanese life, so different from that of all other lands, is not to be found in Europeanized circles. It is to be found among the great common people, who represent in Japan, as in all countries, the national virtues, and who still cling to their delightful old customs, their picturesque dresses, their Buddhist images, their household shrines, their beautiful and touching worship of ancestors. This is the life of which a foreign observer can never weary, if fortunate and sympathetic enough to enter into it—the life that forces him sometimes to doubt whether the course of our boasted Western progress is really in the direction of moral development. (xiii)

A major impetus to the fascination with which Westerners have viewed Japan was Japan's victory over Russia in the Russo–Japanese War (1904–1905). People the world over marveled at how a tiny island country like Japan could win a war against a large and powerful country like Russia (meanwhile wondering about how their own country would fare in war against Japan). At the same time, they wondered about a people who could conquer a nation such as Russia and then allow Russian officials to wear their weapons to the peace treaty ceremony.[2] Partly in response to the request (and even outcry) for knowledge about

Japan at this time came Inazo Nitobe's book, *Bushido: The Soul of Japan* (1969),[3] which attempted to demystify and explain the Japanese character using the concepts of the feudal warrior, or samurai.[4] According to Nitobe, *bushido* can be most closely associated with the English word *chivalry*, and it is this sense of chivalry that permeates the Japanese character.

> Chivalry is a flower no less indigenous to the soil of Japan than its emblem, the cherry blossom; nor is it a dried up specimen of an antique virtue preserved in the herbarium of our history. It is still a loving object of power and beauty among us; and if it assumes no tangible shape or form, it not the less scents *[sic]* the moral atmosphere, and makes us aware that we are still under its potent smell. The conditions of society which brought it forth and nourished it have long disappeared; but as those far-off stars which once were and are not, still continue to shed their rays upon us, so the light of chivalry, which was a child of feudalism, still illuminates our moral path, surviving its mother institution. (1–2)

Bushido was composed of a set of core values that included rectitude or justice, courage, benevolence, politeness, veracity, sincerity, honor, loyalty, and self-control. Many of these are exactly the same values that Hearn had previously written about on his own. Stoicism was also a major part of bushido, as were the concepts of *giri* and *on* (two different types of obligation). Training and education in the bushido way were based on three major principles: wisdom, benevolence, and courage.[5] It is significant that Nitobe, a native Japanese, wrote this work, because it demonstrated consistency between Japanese and non-Japanese writers in their understanding of the essential nature of the Japanese culture and individual. The popularity of Nitobe's book in Japan among Japanese laypersons even today also speaks to this.

World War II stimulated another push to understand Japanese culture, bringing forth Ruth Benedict's 1946 classic in cultural anthropology, *The Chrysanthemum and the Sword*. Benedict's work focused on Japanese values such as giri and on, *chuugi* (loyalty), self-discipline, virtue, honor, and righteousness, especially on the place of these values in the system of ethics and morality in the lives of everyday Japanese. Benedict especially focused on the portrayal of Japan as a "shame culture," where people are motivated by the threat of social isolation or sanction from the people around them. This tendency is related to the notion that the Japanese are group-oriented and that consciousness of and identification with others and with ingroups take precedence. In many ways the content of her work was very similar to the earlier works by Nitobe and Hearn, perhaps partially because during World War II she was assigned to the U.S. Office of War Information to study Japan, thus the obvious links to a warrior code.[6]

Another classic in cultural anthropological studies of Japan is Ronald Dore's book *City Life in Japan* (1958). From his ethnographic study of a neighborhood in Tokyo in which he had lived for several months, Dore wrote about key concepts he considered central to Japanese culture and personality. He focused on the Japanese concept of *seishin*, which is loosely translated as "spirit" or "willpower," and commented that the Japanese belief in seishin and its powers was a core personality trait that permeated Japanese culture. The themes that describe this concept—strength, fortitude, perseverance, single-mindedness, group spirit, self-discipline, loyalty, and devotion—ring a familiar note with Dore's predecessors' descriptions of the nature of Japanese character.[7] These concepts not only described the Japanese; they were the ideals that they strove to achieve, and did, and that set them apart from Westerners.

Another noted Japan scholar, Ivan Morris, wrote a seminal book entitled *The Nobility of Failure* in which he demonstrated that the Japanese view failure, not success, as heroic, and that this is peculiar to the Japanese. Morris understood the tragic side of Japanese culture and used the concept of *makoto* (sincerity) to explain the selflessness and sacrifice of many tragic heroes in Japanese culture. Morris' work was popular not only in the United States but also in Japan, and it maintained the image of the Japanese people and culture as based on values such as makoto.

The works of the authors that have been briefly reviewed here—Hearn, Morris, Nitobe, Dore, and Benedict—are considered by many to be classics in the study of Japanese culture. They share a remarkable degree of similarity in their portrayals of the key moral virtues and values of the Japanese culture and people: humility, perseverance, politeness, modesty, frugality, chivalry, justice, courage, discipline, benevolence, sincerity, honor, loyalty, and self-control. While many of these concepts may have had their roots in the moral and ethical code of the Japanese military class—in bushido—over time they were idealized, ritualized, and institutionalized to become part and parcel of the Japanese cultural landscape. As such, a fairly homogeneous picture of Japanese culture and society emerged, and many Japanese cultural practices in religion, art, music and dance, and other cultural rituals and artifacts were exported around the world as a means by which to instill these types of values and traditions among non-Japanese nations as well.[8] In this way, millions of people around the world were influenced by Japanese culture and society. And these views undoubtedly influenced many contemporary perceptions of Japanese culture and psychology in important and fundamental ways.

Contemporary Views of Japanese Culture

A contributing factor to many of the contemporary works on Japanese culture has been Japan's uncanny rise to economic power after being decimated in World War II. Rising from the ashes, albeit with the necessary aid of foreign intervention, Japan was able to harness all of its people's energy to create what has become the world's second largest economy. In many business areas, Japanese products are second to none, and Japanese innovations, research, and development in various fields of technology continue to lead the world in creating a different and better quality of life for millions.

Thus, interest in and marvel at the Japanese culture and people switched from the battlefield—classic works on Japan's military class and war—to the boardroom. But many authors, in trying to understand and explain Japan's economic feats, retained the stereotypic view of the Japanese culture and people as rather homogeneous and unicultural.

One of the most influential writers in recent history has been Chie Nakane, whose works on Japanese society and culture have furthered the perception that Japanese culture is homogeneous. In her book *Japanese Society* (1970),[9] Nakane focused on the "truly basic components and their potentiality in society—in other words, social persistence" (ix). She suggested that even though Japanese culture and society may change in various ways over time, there are core aspects that have remained the same and that are identifiable.

> The persistence of social structure can be seen clearly in the modes of personal social relation which determine the probable variability of group organization in changing circumstances. This persistence reveals the basic value orientation inherent in society, and is the driving force of the development of society. (ix)

Nakane suggested that the overall structure of Japanese society is not one of horizontal stratification by class or caste, but of vertical stratification by institution or group of institutions. She argued that this social structure is so pervasive in Japan that it results in a quite homogeneous social structure and in considerable similarities in interpersonal relations and individual psychologies (at least in relation to social behavior).

Nakane's analysis of social groups focused on two major points. First, she pointed out that social groups in Japan are formed on the basis of situation, not attributes. Consequently, social groups include members with differing attributes. Group cohesiveness is ensured because even though people may have different attributes, they are led to feel that they are members of the same group (the creation of group identity); this feeling is justified by stressing group consciousness: "us" versus "them."[10]

> Consequently, the power and influence of the group not only affects and enters into the individual's actions; it alters even his ideas and ways of thinking. Individual autonomy is minimized. When this happens, the point where group or public life ends and where private life begins no longer can be distinguished. There are those who perceive this as a danger, an encroachment on their dignity as individuals; on the other hand, others feel safer in total-group consciousness. There seems little doubt that the latter group is in the majority. Their sphere of

> living is usually concentrated solely within the
> village community or place of work. (1970, 10)

Nakane characterized Japanese social groups as family-like, based on the concept of Japanese *ie* (house), and pervasive within the private lives of their members. She suggested that "these characteristics have been cautiously encouraged by managers and administrators consistently from the Meiji Period. And the truth is that this encouragement has always succeeded and reaped rewards" (19).

Nakane's second major point was that Japanese social groups are characterized internally by vertical relationships, oftentimes established through elaborate ranking systems. Once ranking is established, strong emotions tie the hierarchy together through a cultural system of loyalty (chuugi) from the bottom and paternalistic obligation (*onjo-shugi*) from the top. Consequently, Japanese value orientations, according to Nakane, center on loyalty, persistence, perseverance, and obligations, many of the same characteristics that have been espoused previously by influential writers.

Nakane suggested that the cultural composition of Japanese society, combined with the social persistence of these structural elements of society across history, has created a relatively homogeneous Japanese culture and society.

> This structural persistence manifests one of the
> distinctive characteristics of a homogeneous
> society built on a vertical organization principle.
> Such a society is fairly stable; it is difficult to

create revolution or disorder on a national scale,
since there is segmentation of the lower sectors
into various group clusters fenced off from each
other. Structural difficulties stand in the way of a
broad scope of joint activity—members of a trade
union, for example, are too loyal to their own
company to join forces with their brothers in
other company unions; student unions are
unable to muster the great majority of students
but develop groups where the solidarity of one
group differentiates it from another. (1970, 149)

Scholarly literature in sociology, anthropology, psychology, economics, humanities, and literature echoes the images of the Japanese discussed by Nakane. Many scholars have used the concepts described earlier in interpreting Japanese people and culture. Other concepts taken up in contemporary literature on Japan include discipline (*kiritsu*), order (*chitsujo*), meekness (*sunao*), and goodwill (*koui*), all of which are related, at least to some degree, to previous conceptualizations about Japan. As portrayals of this type became increasingly popular over the years, the Japanese people and culture became synonymous with them.

Even relatively recent writing by noted scholars and authorities on Japan continues to portray Japanese people and culture as homogeneous. Edwin Reischauer, for example, in his 1988 book entitled *The Japanese Today: Change and Continuity,* commented about the self-sacrificing and unselfish nature of the Japanese people toward groups.

Various societies differ greatly in the relative emphasis placed on the individual and the group. Certainly no difference is more significant between Japanese and Americans, or Westerners in general, than the greater Japanese tendency to emphasize the group at the expense of the individual…. The key Japanese value is harmony, which they seek to achieve by a subtle process of mutual understanding, almost by intuition, rather than by a sharp analysis of conflicting views or by clear-cut decisions, whether made by one-man dictates or majority votes. (128, 136)

Although Nakane's *Japanese Society*, described above, was originally published in 1970, her views on the homogeneity of Japanese culture and society were essentially unchanged even twenty-seven years later.

In the prehistoric period, the Japanese islands were covered by a single cultural type known as Jomon culture. There were also minority groups of people known as Ainu and Ezo. But they have mixed extensively with the majority of Japanese. Thus considered from a broader view, only a single ethnic group has occupied Japan for a very long time.

Later, rice growing was initiated under the influence of the Asian continent. The rice-planting culture quickly spread throughout Japan, resulting in the creation of a national culture based on wet-paddy cultivation.

Looking at the various other nations of the world, both in Europe and Asia, it is hard to find another nation in which the entire population is included in such a common culture. In other

words, Japan is an unusually homogeneous
society. If Japan is approached for *[sic]* this point
of view, it may be surprisingly easy to understand. (1997, 181–83)

The Publisher's Foreword to the 1976 reprinting
of Lafcadio Hearn's 1894 work also promulgated the
stereotypic view of the homogeneous and unicultural
Japanese society.

Even though much has changed in Japan since
he [Hearn] came under the spell of that country,
what he had to say about it still has a remarkable
validity, for the Japanese spirit has changed
considerably less than the material conditions of
Japanese life. In a word, the Japanese character
and the Japanese tradition are still fundamentally
the same as Hearn found them to be, and for
this reason his books are still extremely revealing
to readers in the West. (ix)

A surprising amount of comparative American-
Japanese research exists. Recently, I did a computer
search for comparative studies in the fields of psychology and communication alone, and found well
over one thousand citations for works published over
the past twenty years or so. I certainly have not read
all of them, but I have read a fair portion and have
found that all of those, to a fault, describe Japanese
culture the same way as described here. When differences between Americans and Japanese are found,
such differences are said to exist because the Japanese are group-oriented and interdependent; because

they value harmony, cooperation, and cohesion; and because they suppress their true feelings.

In short, Japanese culture and people are portrayed in academic circles today in a fashion similar to the way they were portrayed in the writings of Hearn, Benedict, Dore, Morris, Nakane, Nitobe, Reischauer, and every other leading Japanologist. If contemporary views of Japanese culture are not exactly the same as those held one hundred or more years ago, they are logical extensions of them (e.g., collectivism may not have been discussed as such, but the current focus on Japanese collectivism may be viewed as an extension of previous views of loyalty, sincerity, sacrifice, etc.).[11] These stereotypic images of the Japanese culture and people are no longer merely stereotypes; they *are* the Japanese.

Japanese Culture in the Media

These stereotyped depictions of the Japanese exist not only in the scholarly literature; they are also promulgated via movies and other media. One relatively recent film, *Rising Sun*, portrays the Japanese as doing whatever they can for the sake of the company—even covering up a murder and keeping special housing for mistresses (group consciousness, collectivism, sacrifice). The movie depicts the Japanese workers as rigid, disciplined, austere, and all-obedient to the elder statesman chairman of the board (loyalty, filial piety, obligations). There is a martial-arts-like quality to the manners, etiquette, and respect displayed by the subordinates in the movie (politeness, meekness, sincerity), and some of the main Japanese characters are skilled in karate (as if all Japanese people are proficient in martial arts). Although the cultural attributes are translated to the contemporary corporate world, the underlying image of the Japanese is the same—that of the bushido warrior.

Even some recent writings on Japanese economics and business management call the Japanese company workers (salarymen) "samurai in suits." This image is promulgated by almost every type of communication and information resource that exists—scholarly and popular books, academic journal writing, business and practical books, movies, magazines, television, and the like.

Within the Japanese media, who can doubt the long-standing popularity of the movies and books commonly known as *Chuushingura* (the story of the forty-seven ronin) or the "nobility of failure" in the stories of Tora-san (*Otoko wa tsurai yo*, literally "Men Have a Hard Life" or, more simply "What a Life"), whose movies graced theaters and televisions on New Year's in Japan for years? The Chuushingura stories are not only an interesting description of history; they have come to idealize the character and virtue the Japanese want to ascribe to themselves. The poignancy of the forty-seven ronin is yet another example of the warrior code that many Japanese revere and identify with, as are many of the images from the mass media.

Japanese Culture as Viewed by Japanese

Many Japanese scholars have used religion in attempting to explain the origins of the Japanese culture and spirit. The origins of Buddhism and Shintoism and the teachings of Confucius are often used as a base from which core Japanese values—hierarchical relationships, cooperation, group harmony, filial piety, and the like—have been ingrained in the Japanese for hundreds or thousands of years. Other scholars continue to use the concept of bushido to explain the Japanese culture and character.

Japanese psychologists have described the psychological nature of the Japanese. Hiroshi Minami, for example, proposed three aspects of the Japanese—inner, outer, and active. The inner aspect includes faint-heartedness, shyness, reserve, and resignation. The outer aspect contains such traits as consideration, gentleness, and kindness. The active aspect refers to studiousness, aspiration, and work discipline. Minami's theory provides an organizational framework for the core psychological characteristics that we have been discussing throughout this chapter.[12]

Another well-known psychologist is Takeo Doi, who wrote a book entitled *The Anatomy of Dependence (Amae no Kouzou)*. In this book Doi suggested that interdependence (*amae*) is a basic value of Japanese people. This concept has been used to explain collectivism and group harmony, as amae is at the core of group consciousness in Japan.

Some writers have suggested that collectivism and group harmony are fixed patterns of character—archetypes—that are unconscious and that cut across historical generations. These writers use the concept of archetypes first suggested by the psychoanalyst Carl Jung to suggest that these archetypes are a collective part of the Japanese personality and an indisputable aspect of Japanese character.

Finally, some Japanese writers have described how the value of harmony, or *wa*, was added to the Constitution of Seventeen Articles by Crown Prince Shotoku, according to the Nihon shoki (a historical-mythological document explaining the origin of Japan). Values such as harmony and collectivism are viewed as inherent aspects of the Japanese spirit and are keys to distinguishing the culture of Japan from that of China or India.

These views are not limited to academics. I come across many students from Japan who are studying in the United States in fields such as psychology or communication. They often base their research on these same images and stereotypes of Japan. These students—born and raised in Japan—view Japan as a land of makoto, sunao, *gaman* (patience, tolerance), *shinbou* (perseverance, endurance), and the like.

Undoubtedly, Japanese people think about Japan in this way partly because they want to and partly because these notions are ingrained in them from early on. There is nobility in these descriptions, and the Japanese themselves actively promote the inherent goodness of their images of themselves, even if they know that the reality may be different.

Allow me to recap these values and virtues that are common to the warrior class, that so aptly describe all of Japanese culture, character, personality, and people. They include rectitude or *gi* (justice), *yuu* (courage), *jin* (benevolence), *rei* (politeness), makoto (veracity and sincerity), *meiyo* (honor), chuugi (loyalty), and *kokki* (self-control). These are the values that, according to Japanese and Westerners alike, describe Japanese culture.[13]

In summary, stereotypic views about Japanese culture are promulgated not only by Westerners but also by Japanese scholars, writers, and the Japanese public. This is what the Japanese want to think about themselves, and this is how they want to portray themselves to the rest of the world.

Stability in Contemporary Japanese Society

As the world collectively holds on to these stereotypic views about Japanese culture and society, contemporary Japan seems plagued with a sense of confusion, unrest, and anxiety, which raises questions about the veracity of these comfortable and familiar views today. An increasing number of people in Japan are worried and confused about their lives, society, and culture. The picture of contemporary Japanese culture and society painted not only by anecdotal and personal experiences but also by objective data provides a stark contrast to the picture of the homogeneous, collective, and harmonious Japanese society of the past.

For example, the Japanese government has periodically commissioned large-scale surveys of the general population in order to gain a sense of the pulse of the general public. One such survey was conducted in 1999 (*Kokumin Seikatsu Hakusho*), and the results were reported to the Japanese Cabinet (10 December 1999) by the Economic Planning Agency (EPA) of the Japanese government.[14] An overwhelming majority of the more than three thousand Japanese participants reported considerably negative views on contemporary Japanese society (Figure 1.1, page 22).

The *Asahi Shimbun* (newspaper) also conducted an annual face-to-face survey on similar issues related to the Japanese public's views on contemporary society. In one survey conducted in December, 1997, three thousand individuals (2,314 respondents) were asked to select the single word they thought best described current society.[15] The word selected most often by the respondents was *confusion* (32%), followed by *unfair* (18%), *selfish* (17%), and *decadence* (11%). Only 7 percent of the respondents said that they viewed society as *stable*.

The *Asahi Shimbun* conducted another face-to-face survey of Japanese individuals on their opinions about life under recession in 1998. The survey was conducted in March with three thousand randomly selected voters (2,211 respondents). Their outlook, in general, was

Figure 1.1*
Japanese People's Views on Contemporary Society

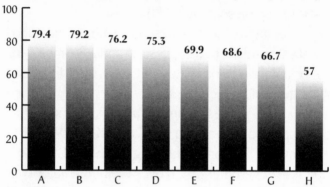

Percentage of people who responded that

A There are many irresponsible
people.

B Everyone acts selfishly.

C Everyone is too busy to relax.

D Social justice and a sense of
morality are declining.

E Society is buffeted by changes.

F People are cold toward others.

G Public morals are corrupt.

H There are many uncertainties.

not positive, as most individuals surveyed (75%) reported anxiety concerning what is known as the "Big
Bang," a term given to the government's attempt to create financial system reform in order to revitalize the
economy. By making the Japanese financial market
commensurate with the international markets of New
York and London, Japan began to engage in planning
that would bring about major changes in areas such as
financial services, securities, insurance, real estate, and
the like. These impending changes, of course, brought
about uncertainty and anxiety among the Japanese
people, which were reflected in the survey data.

---

* See page ix for a statement regarding figures.

Needless to say, such anticipation of large-scale financial changes forced people to rethink their way of life, which in fact has major implications for social and cultural change. A full 59 percent of the people surveyed in the 1998 *Asahi Shimbun* survey reported that they were seriously reconsidering their way of life because of the current situation in Japan.

In a separate study comparing youth aged fourteen to eighteen in Japan and Finland (conducted by Komazawa Women's University, the NHK [Nihon Housou Kyoukai] Research Institute in Japan, and Finland Gallup in 1995), 2,989 Japanese teenagers and a comparable number of Finnish teenagers were asked about their attitudes toward the future outlook of their country over the next ten years.[16] Most of the Japanese teenagers reported that they were "not very hopeful" or "not hopeful at all" (see Figure 1.2 in the Appendix). The comparison with the Finnish youth data is startling.

When the Japanese youth were queried in more detail about their responses, they indicated that they were fairly certain that, relative to past trends, Japan's course would take a turn for the worse over the next ten years. Seventy-eight percent of them believed that the environment will become even more polluted than it is now; 65 percent believed that crime and violence will worsen; 54 percent believed that social security protections will weaken; and 53 percent believed that the employment situation will worsen.

Even Japanese responses to emerging technologies had a negative flavor. This is surprising because Japan is a world leader in technology, and the Japanese public makes great use of technological advances in their everyday lives. For example, in the 1997 *Asahi Shimbun* opinion poll, people were asked about their reactions to improving and emerging technologies in the workplace. While many responded that computers and other technologies did make things more convenient and business more effective, 31 percent said that they either could not keep up with those changes or might lose their jobs because of them. While not a majority, these people represent such a large percentage that their attitudes cannot be ignored.

Even in an international comparison of attitudes toward the merits of advancing information technology conducted by the EPA (with three thousand respondents in Japan aged eighteen to sixty-nine years), the Japanese consistently had the least positive outlook of the countries surveyed: Japan, United States, England, France, and Germany (Figure 1.3, page 25).

Perhaps some of the most telling statistics regarding the current tenor of attitudes in Japan come from Ed Diener and Shigehiro Oishi's (2000) study of subjective well-being across forty-two countries. Subjective well-being (SWB) refers to the degree to which people evaluate their lives in a positive fashion. The greater the SWB, the more positive they feel about the quality of their lives. Diener and his colleagues have developed a method for measuring SWB reliably, validly, and cross-culturally and have used this measure

Figure 1.3
Comparison of the Merits of Information Technology

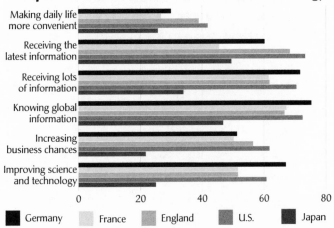

in numerous studies in many different countries. In their most recent work, they examined the relationship in each of the forty-two countries between the average SWB and national income, as measured by purchasing power parity in U.S. dollars. Even though their results indicated a fairly strong and consistent correlation between income and SWB across all countries, closer inspection of the data indicated that of the eight countries with the highest national income, Japan had the lowest average SWB score (Table 1.1, page 26).

These data are even more remarkable when one considers how economic growth may be related to SWB over time. Diener and Oishi examined the relationship between these two variables across time in fifteen countries. Data from Japan were collected over twenty-two years, during which time Japan experienced an average of 4.1 percent economic growth per annum, the highest of all of the countries included in the comparison. However, Japan's SWB scores showed virtually no relationship to the growth.[17]

Table 1.1
National Income of Top Eight Countries and SWB Scores[18]

Country	Income	Life Satisfaction
Luxembourg	$28,770	0.68
United States	$25,860	0.78
Switzerland	$25,150	1.38
Japan	$21,350	-0.90
Iceland	$21,150	0.97
Norway	$21,120	0.80
Denmark	$20,800	1.28
Belgium	$20,270	0.70

Statistics compiled by various agencies of the Japanese government also raise questions about contemporary culture and society. As much of the public already knows, the number of all crimes reported, as well as the number of arrests made by police, has risen steadily since 1984; and deaths due to certain diseases such as cancer and heart disease have also risen since the 1950s. Increases in both of these areas are to be expected because, during the same time, the population has grown considerably, in sync, actually, with the rates of increase in overall crime and deaths due to cancer and heart disease. Yet, two statistical findings are of note to our discussion here.

First, while the rise in overall crime is consonant with increases in the general population, the case of felony offenses stands out. From 1984 to 1989 felony offenses actually *decreased* every year in Japan. But in the ten-year span from 1989 to 1999, felony offenses increased dramatically, almost doubling. Thus, relative to the data for previous felony offenses, the change in these statistics during that ten-year period is alarming. The fact that these offenses tend to be the most morally reprehensible speaks volumes concerning the possible changes in social and cultural fabric of the country; these crimes are lamented in the newspapers, television, and print media in Japan almost daily.

Second, the fact that deaths due to cancer and heart disease have increased, while at the same time those due to cerebrovascular disease have decreased, is indicative of a trend toward increasing individualism in the culture. In a study conducted by my laboratory (Matsumoto and Fletcher 1996), we found that individualistic cultures are associated with higher degrees of heart disease and cancer, while collectivistic cultures are associated with higher incidences of cerebrovascular diseases. The changes in incidence rates of these diseases in Japan, therefore, are congruent with the notion of a changing culture.

Collectively, then, the figures in this section reflect a growing degree of unrest, dissatisfaction, and anxiety among many Japanese people. These data run contrary to the popular, stereotypic beliefs about Japanese culture and society. What's going on?

The Causes for This Degree of Unrest

Clearly, there are no easy answers to the question of what is going on in Japan to cause such unrest. The causes, in fact, are multiple and include political, social, economic, and psychological factors, all of which interact to produce a unique experience for Japanese individuals—the blending of traditional and contemporary characteristics of society.

In this book, I explore one of these factors—the changes in Japanese culture and society and the consequences of these changes on the psychology of Japanese individuals. In short, I believe that deepseated changes in Japanese culture and society are creating a stressful environment in which people must live and function. Those changes then lead to feelings of dissatisfaction, unrest, anxiety, and apprehension about the future. I believe that cultural duality, not homogeneity, exists in Japan today and that previous stereotypic conceptualizations of Japanese culture are simply not adequate representations of the values, attitudes, and beliefs of large segments of the current Japanese population.

In this book I will show how Japanese culture is undergoing a major evolution, thereby creating a heterogeneous society with multiple cultures. In particular I will show that the cultural values held by many of the younger generations (i.e., under thirty-five years of age) in Japan are considerably different from those held by their elders—and from the predominant stereotypes of Japanese cultural and moral values. In many societies such cultural changes can be interpreted as merely a "generation gap" between older and younger individuals in the society. In Japan, too, the predominant belief until now has been that upon graduation from college and entrance into a company, the Japanese individual becomes a *shakaijin* (person of society), and the Japanese companies and various organizations work to resocialize the Japanese individual into the dominant Japanese cultural mores and norms.[19] I, however, believe these sociocultural changes to be major and pervasive, permeating many strata of society, and not "fixed" by a readjustment upon employment. These changes have, in fact, forced differences in attitudes concerning education, personnel and human resources decisions within Japanese companies, and everyday life in Japan.

Nakane (1970) wrote that Japanese culture is surprisingly easy to understand. As it stands today, however, I believe that Japanese culture may be one of the most difficult to understand because of the combination of influences it must reconcile: traditional, historical aspects of Japanese culture; the influx and influence of other cultures; the advent of technology; the changing population density and sociodemographic characteristics; and affluence. These factors interact to produce a unique contemporary culture that cannot be pigeonholed into an easy-to-understand format. How can one understand the image of girls in traditional kimonos on *seijin shiki*[20] day walking down the street, their cellular phones ringing with the melodies of a popular musician. Such cultural clashes are apparent everywhere in Japan today.

In the next chapter I will provide data about seven selected stereotypes of Japanese culture to demonstrate how Japanese culture has changed drastically. I will then discuss why these changes have occurred and their implications for business, school, sports, and everyday life. Quite frankly, much of the strain people experience today is, in my opinion, the result of opposing cultural values held by large segments of the population, the stress that is created by a cultural duality, and the resulting social and psychological consequences. I will conclude the book by giving some thought to what the future may hold for Japan as it negotiates these changes, evolving into a different and, I hope, better Japan, striving for a brighter future for its children.

Textnotes

[1] Of course the Meiji Restoration represented much more than political overthrow and change at a single time. The year attributed to the Restoration, 1868, represented the point in time when social and cultural unrest, combined with increased pressure from outside Japan, came to a head after years of simmering. Whether the Restoration represented a revolution in the European or American sense has been debated among historians. For more information on the history of the Restoration and these issues, consult Hall (1968) and Hall and Jansen (1968).

2 The surrender of the Russian Army at Port Arthur in 1905 was photographed and depicts this scene, which by some accounts was unheard-of in the European history of warfare.

3 The English version published by Tuttle lists the original publication date as 1905. The original Japanese edition, however, lists the publication date as 1899.

4 Apparently, Nitobe wrote the book partly to describe the Japanese culture to his American wife, Mary, who had asked many questions of her Japanese husband about the Japanese character, and partly to satisfy requests from professional colleagues. With the close of the Russo–Japanese War in 1905, the book became popular, explaining what was unique about the Japanese that enabled the country to be victorious.

5 It is interesting to compare Nitobe's account of bushido with that of earlier writings, such as Tsunetomo Yamamoto's *Hagakure: The Book of the Samurai*, originally written over a period of seven years, from 1710 to 1716. The principles of the way of the warrior as espoused in this work are fundamentally different from those described by Nitobe. In *Hagakure* there is a profound emphasis on two major issues: one's attitude toward death and loyalty to one's master. Although other concepts and values, such as those mentioned by Nitobe and others, are mentioned in various places in this collection of writings, they are strongly overshadowed by the two major concepts. I interpret the differences existing between these two major pieces of writing to be a product of Japan's history. *Hagakure* was written before the end of Japan's Warring Period (Sengoku Jidai) and well within memory of the Shimabara rebellion in 1638. Thus, the principles of the *bushi* as expounded in this writing were more extreme, raw if you will, when death in battle was viewed as honorable. "Merit lies more in dying for one's master than in striking down the enemy" (1979, 55) is a theme that appears consistently throughout *Hagakure*.

When Nitobe's *Bushido* was written, however, Japan had been at peace for three centuries. As wars and battles were nonexistent, the moral code of the warrior evolved from an emphasis on battle to a focus on a warrior's way of life. As such, the view of bushido came to be idealized. Thus, the moral codes and values described by Nitobe read much like a stylized code of ethics because in a great sense that is exactly what they had become.

6 Another reason why her work reflects much of the traditional, stereotypic views of Japan is, I believe, because unlike most writers of cultural anthropology, she was unable to visit and live in Japan and experience the country first-hand and in-depth because of the war. Thus, primary resources were interviews with Japanese Americans, current events, and published works on Japanese culture and people. Reliance on self-reports instead of actual observations and experiences of Japanese life may in fact foster a stereotypic view of a culture. Such self-reports, especially concerning Japan, may tend to be as much social (re)construction as they are objective indices about Japanese culture and lifestyle. The interviewees studied and the reports read may have led to the glossy, stereotypic picture of the Japanese in *The Chrysanthemum and the Sword*.

There are also several other issues to consider. First the Japanese Americans who were available for Benedict to interview had in fact left Japan for one reason or another, and, while they may have been born in Japan, they may not have been representative of Japanese in Japan (Takaki 1989).

Second, during World War II many Japanese immigrants and their families were interned in camps. It is not known what influence this life experience may have had on the reports of Japanese culture the interviewees may have given. These two issues, therefore, suggest the potential for a sampling bias among the interviewees utilized by

Benedict in her research. That Japanese in Japan have marveled at the "accuracy" of Benedict's work is not surprising, though, as her stereotypic notion of the Japanese culture and character is essentially perpetuated by Japanese writers as well.

7 See a review of Dore's *City Life in Japan* and a related work by Brian Moeran (1986).

8 One of these cultural imports is the art and sport of judo and its derivative, jujitsu. The spread of jujitsu and judo around the world coincided with the heightened interest in Japanese bushido. Demonstrations, championships, matches, and seminars were established around the world by leading Japanese instructors of judo and jujitsu. The spread of such Japanese cultural artifacts is quite astonishing; today, for example, judo is one of the most popular, well-practiced sports in the world, with one of the largest international sports organizations in the International Olympic Committee (currently 183 countries are official members of the International Judo Federation).

9 Japanese readers may also want to see her *Tate-shakai no ningen-kankei: Tanitsu-shakai no riron* (*Personal Relations in a Vertical Society: A Theory of Homogeneous Society*). 1967. Tokyo: Kodansha.

10 See also the Triandis et al. (1988) article on differences in ingroup and outgroup relationships between individualistic and collectivistic cultures.

11 This point is important, as much of the data I present in chapter 2 speak directly to collectivism and its opposite, individualism.

12 Minami also suggested that because these three aspects of the Japanese personality are such strong components of the Japanese character, the Japanese have a basic uncertainty of the self—who they are—because who they are depends on which aspect of the self they happen to be in at the time.

[13] To be sure, Westerners also have negative stereotypes of the Japanese. For example, many individuals, dating from Hearn's writing, comment on the "inscrutability" of the Japanese. Related to perceptions of inscrutability are images of the Japanese as sly, sneaky, untrustworthy. Such negative images have been considered by some to be at the root of discriminatory practices against the Japanese and Japanese Americans (e.g., see the literature on Japanese internment camps during World War II, or Shintaro Ishihara's [1989] book entitled *The Japan that Can Say No*).

[14] www.epa.go.jp

[15] Kanzaki.com/jpoll/regular97.html

[16] www.freenet.hut.fi/monitoimitalo/nuoriso/chapter6.html

[17] To be sure, the degree of relationship between national economic growth and SWB was virtually nonexistent for all the countries studied. This suggests that, on average, people do not report being happier despite the availability of more goods and services.

[18] Life Satisfaction scores are expressed as standardized scores, with a mean of 0 and standard deviation of 1. The negative score for Japan indicates that the Japanese SWB score is almost 1 standard deviation below the average of all countries compared. "Income" purchasing power parity in U.S. dollars where available and GNP elsewhere.

[19] For example, Nakane (1970) wrote,

It is often agreed that, in these "modern" days, the younger generation tends to infringe the rules of order. But it is interesting to note that young people soon begin to follow the traditional order once they are employed, as they gradually realize the social cost that such infringement involves. (32)

[20] *Seijin shiki* is an annual "coming of age" event where children are, at the age of twenty, officially recognized as adults.

2

Seven Stereotypes about Japanese Culture and Their Reality

In this chapter I discuss seven well-known and well-accepted stereotypes about Japanese culture and society and present evidence from research that suggests they are not adequate representations of Japanese culture today. Some of the research I review comes from contemporary psychological research, published in scholarly, peer-reviewed journals; other data come from surveys conducted within Japan by the government or the private sector, such as those introduced in the second half of chapter 1. All of the research reviewed, regardless of its source, involves as participants Japanese individuals born and raised in Japan and does not include Japanese Americans or other Japanese immigrant groups found outside Japan.

The studies that come from research published in peer-reviewed journals typically involve university students as participants. Other studies reviewed, however, involve nonstudent samples and span a wide range of ages of people in Japan. This point is important because some people believe that the cultural changes we are witness to today are limited to university student samples, the typical participants in psychological research. If you *only* view research results published in peer-reviewed journals and consider nothing else, this may be a plausible argument. I believe, however, that findings from the business and marriage studies described below, which are based on samples of Japanese participants of different ages, amply suggest that what we are observing is not limited to university students. Instead, these data indicate that a true cultural evolution is occurring in Japan. A new, qualitatively and meaningfully different culture is emerging. What we are observing in our everyday lives in Japan is not a fad or a generation gap that the youth will "get over," but are signs of real and drastic changes in the culture of this society.

The evidence, therefore, forcefully challenges the validity of stereotypic notions about Japanese culture and society, rendering them more myth than truth, more fantasy than reality. Although discussion of only seven aspects of Japanese culture is not at all comprehensive, I do believe these aspects are at the heart of deep-seated changes in the very fabric of society and point to the fact that Japan is in the midst of a huge transformation whereby multiple cultural groups are being created.

Stereotype 1: Japanese Collectivism

Background

One of the most common stereotypes that Japanese and non-Japanese alike have about Japanese culture concerns the cultural dimension known as *collectivism* and its counterpart, *individualism*. Cultural psychologists and anthropologists have used this construct for years to describe cultural differences in self-other relationships across different societies of the world.

Basically, individualism and collectivism reflect the degree to which individuals in any society identify with, sacrifice themselves for, and otherwise coexist with others around them. On the one hand, individualistic cultures foster the needs, wishes, and desires of individuals over their ingroups (see discussion of ingroups and outgroups below). As such, they value competition, uniqueness, and separateness. The United States, Australia, and Great Britain are commonly thought to be individualistic societies. In these cultures individuals are valued, as are autonomy and independence. Such values manifest themselves in a variety of ways: child rearing (e.g., getting children to sleep in their own room as soon as possible), education, and employment. As it is said in the U.S., "The squeaky wheel gets the grease," and those who stand out reap many social benefits.

Collectivistic cultures, on the other hand, foster the needs, wishes, and desires of ingroups over individuals. They foster values such as cooperation, harmony, and conformity. In such cultures people are expected to "go with the flow," sacrifice their personal aspirations and desires for the sake of the common good, and maintain a strong group identity.

To understand how individualism and collectivism affect social behavior, we must also discuss the sociological concept known as ingroups and outgroups. People in all societies categorize others in their social sphere; it is a natural, necessary, and normal part of social behavior. Ingroup relationships are those that are characterized by familiarity, intimacy, a shared history, and potential future relationships. Typical ingroups include family, close friends, loved ones, work colleagues, peers, and the like. Outgroup relationships, however, are characterized by unfamiliarity, a lack of intimacy and emotional ties, and distance. Typical outgroup others include strangers, casual acquaintances, and the like.

The relationship between the self and ingroup/ outgroup members differs according to individualism and collectivism. In individualistic cultures, people tend to make fewer distinctions between ingroups and outgroups, because of the emphasis on individuals rather than groups. In collectivistic cultures, however, people tend to make greater distinctions between ingroups and outgroups, because of the importance attached to the relationship of the self to the ingroup.

The strong distinction between ingroups and outgroups actually helps to maintain ingroup harmony and cohesion. This tendency is considered an essential part of collectivism; in collectivistic societies ingroups are much more sacred and protected than in individualistic societies. In collectivistic societies one belongs to fewer ingroups, but the ties to, identification with, and psychological importance of those ingroups are stronger than in individualistic societies.

Over the years many writers have referred to the Japanese culture as collectivistic, as described in chapter 1. Many of the classical writings about Japanese culture, for example, describe the importance of the group over individual needs and use terms such as loyalty, filial piety, obligation, and sacrifice to describe many of the main values of Japanese culture. Contemporary works by Chie Nakane, Edwin Reischauer, and others also paint a similar picture of Japanese cultural values centering on collectivism.

The Evidence

In fact this stereotypic view of Japanese culture as collectivistic received some scientific support in a large-scale study on values in the workplace by organizational scientist Geert Hofstede over thirty years ago (1980; 1984).[1] In his study, managers and other employees of a large, international business firm (the identity of which was originally concealed but was later revealed as IBM) completed a large survey on their attitudes, beliefs, and values about work. The respondents included employees from subsidiaries in approximately fifty countries around the world, involving literally thousands of respondents. Hofstede analyzed the data and found that one of the dimensions that differentiated the responses was individualism versus collectivism. When he placed the countries in order according to this dimension, Hofstede found that the United States was at the far end of individualistic cultures, while Japan ranked toward the middle (i.e., much more collectivistic).

Despite this early support for the stereotype concerning Japanese collectivism and American individualism, there has been no support for this distinction in recent psychological research directly testing this notion. In fact since Hofstede's original study, seventeen other studies have been conducted directly examining Japanese collectivism and American individualism, and *not one has supported this claim*.[2]

For example, my laboratory conducted a study in which we asked 138 American and 137 Japanese university students to complete a test for individualism and collectivism (Matsumoto et al. 1997b). This test included over one hundred questions, was based on years of work in the field, and has been reliably used in a number of studies concerning this cultural dimension. When we tested for differences between the two groups on their overall individualism–collectivism scores, we found no differences.

Other researchers have reported similar results. For example, Kim Carter and Dale Dinnel tested American and Japanese university students on two scales designed to measure collectivistic attitudes and values (Carter and Dinnel 1997). On the Collectivism Scale, there was no discernible difference between the Americans and Japanese. On the Collectivistic Values Index scale, the Americans actually scored higher than the Japanese on collectivism (see Figure 2.1 in the Appendix). This suggests that not only is the stereotype concerning Japanese collectivism not supported, but in fact the opposite may be true—the Japanese may actually be less collectivistic, that is, more individualistic than are Americans.

Japanese psychologists interested in individualism and collectivism have also reported similar findings. For instance, Susumu Yamaguchi, a social psychologist at the University of Tokyo, and his colleagues studied collectivism in Japan, Korea, and the United States (Yamaguchi, Kuhlman, and Sugimori 1995). These researchers asked 238 American (146 in Delaware and 92 in Washington), 295 Japanese, and 293 Korean university students to complete a scale designed to measure collectivism. When the researchers analyzed the data for differences among the countries, they found, to their surprise, no differences between the American and Japanese students on collectivism. This finding also provides no support for the contention that Japanese individuals are more collectivistic than Americans. (The Korean students, however, were significantly more collectivistic than both the Americans and the Japanese; see Figure 2.2 in the Appendix.)

When various aspects of collectivism and individualism are studied separately, the findings are even more revealing. For example, in the study conducted by my laboratory that was described earlier (Matsumoto et al. 1997b), we asked American, Japanese, Korean, and Russian university students to complete a test of individualistic and collectivistic values in relation to their interactions with their family members. Many social scientists, Japanese and non-Japanese alike, have often described the importance of the nuclear family as the most stable and prototypical example of collectivistic values and behaviors in Asian cultures. These stereotypes no doubt owe some of their origin to the importance of the family and family structure in Confucian teachings, as well as in religions such as Buddhism, Shintoism, and Taoism, all of which have a major influence over Japanese and other Asian cultures.[3] Thus, I predicted that the Korean and Japanese students would have the highest collectivism scores in relation to interactions with their families, while Russians and Americans would have the lowest.

The data, however, proved otherwise. Koreans did have relatively high collectivism scores in relation to their families (4.39). But Russian students had the highest collectivism scores (4.41), and both Russians and Americans (4.10) had significantly higher collectivism scores than the Japanese (3.41), who had the lowest scores on this scale (see Figure 2.3 in the Appendix). These data indicate that of the four countries surveyed, the Japanese had the lowest collectivistic attitudes, values, and beliefs toward their families, which runs contrary to prevalent notions of Japanese ie and collectivism.[4] And these differences were quite substantial.

Japanese relationships between the self and outgroups also do not conform to the stereotypic notion of such relationships in collectivistic societies. As I discussed earlier in this section, strangers are a prototypical outgroup category, and collectivistic cultures foster fundamentally different relationships with outgroup "others" than do individualistic cultures; in supposedly collectivistic cultures such as Japan, individuals make large distinctions between ingroups and outgroups. In the past Japan was said to have a society that was relatively closed to outsiders, one in which it was difficult to gain entrance to an ingroup. In individualistic cultures such as the United States, people have apparently made less differentiation between ingroups and outgroups because people are viewed as individuals first, not as agents of a group.

Yet, data from the Matsumoto (1997b) study concerning collectivistic values toward strangers—clearly an outgroup category—do not support this contention. One would expect that the Japanese and Koreans would have relatively low scores here, because collectivistic societies would encourage *less* tolerant or friendly (collectivistic) attitudes and behaviors toward people who are clearly outsiders. The Americans and Russians, on the other hand, would be thought to have relatively higher scores. But the Russians and Japanese had the highest collectivism scores in relation to strangers, while Americans had the lowest. This suggested that the Japanese made fewer differentiations between ingroups and outgroups than did the Americans, which is exactly contrary to the stereotypic belief about entrance to groups in supposedly collectivistic cultures such as Japan (see Figure 2.4 in the Appendix). Again, the size of the difference obtained here was substantial.

These findings exist not only in studies in social psychology involving questionnaires, but also in research examining actual behaviors. Japanese psychologist Toshio Yamagishi, for example, conducted two studies in which American and Japanese students participated in small monocultural groups that required cooperative behavior to perform a task (1988a; 1988b). When a system of mutual monitoring and social sanctions existed for individual participation in the group, the Japanese students did indeed contribute more to the group than did the Americans. But, when the system of monitoring and sanctions was eliminated, it was the Americans, not the Japanese, who contributed more. In fact more Japanese chose to leave the group than did Americans. American participants had higher levels of trust and cooperation in the unmonitored setting. These findings imply that Japanese cooperative behavior in group settings may be limited to certain types of contexts, especially those in which one's behavior is monitored and reinforced. When such external constraints do not exist, Americans exhibit higher degrees of cooperative behavior than the Japanese. Clearly, these types of findings, like those described above involving questionnaires, challenge the stereotype of Japanese collectivism and American individualism.[5]

In an earlier study conducted by my research lab, I estimated the percentage of Japanese individuals who demonstrate not only collectivistic/individualistic behavior but also values and attitudes. In that study, for example, I classified Japanese university students based on their responses to an individualism versus collectivism questionnaire (Matsumoto, Kudoh, and Takeuchi 1996). The results were impressive (see Figure 2.5).

Figure 2.5
Individualists and Collectivists among
Japanese Students

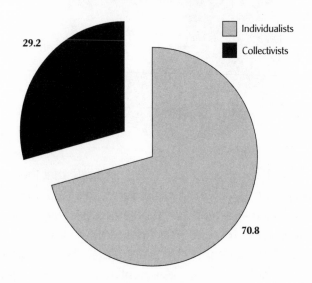

29.2

70.8

Individualists

Collectivists

In the same study we compared the Japanese university students' responses with those of Japanese working adults whose average age was thirty-nine. We classified the adults as either individualists or collectivists, depending on their responses on the questionnaire, using the same criteria as for the students. The results from the adult sample were contrary to those of the students (see Figure 2.6).

Figure 2.6
Individualists and Collectivists among Japanese Adults

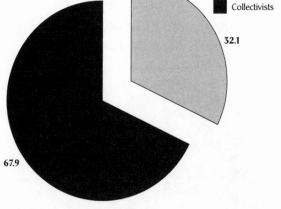

The data reported here clearly indicate that there is a major rift between the cultural values of Japanese youth, exhibited by the data from university student samples in numerous social psychology studies, and those of mainstream Japanese culture. These findings are not a fluke; they are consistent across many studies and different methodologies—both questionnaire and actual behavioral and laboratory studies—conducted by both Japanese and non-Japanese researchers.

Some people may believe that these data are indicative of just a fad or a generation gap of some sort. They generally suggest that once Japanese youth became socialized after graduation from the university and enter the workforce (*shakaijin*), they are once again initiated and socialized into Japanese cultural ways, by companies and society as a whole.

There is certainly some truth to this notion, and the data presented immediately above could be interpreted as part of that phenomenon. While this notion of reculturation may have been accurate in the past,[6] I do not believe that it can account fully or satisfactorily for the data described here or for many of the other changes in Japanese culture that I report below as well. I believe these data indicate that Japanese culture and society are clearly in transition, with major and widespread differences in beliefs, values, attitudes, and behaviors among individuals and groups. Quite frankly, the data argue against the stereotypic notion of Japanese collectivism, at least among the younger generations, and speak directly to the existence of at least two groups in Japan with quite different cultural value systems.

Stereotype 2: Japanese Self-Concepts

Background

In social and personality psychology, one of the most

interesting and frequently researched areas of study is self-concept. In psychology the self is thought to be a center for organizing and monitoring behaviors, perceptions, attitudes, beliefs, and individual differences. Self-concepts are used to describe people's personality traits and characteristics and can also be called self-descriptors or self-construals.

The study of the self and self-concepts has had a long history in the field of psychology in the United States and Europe. Because it has been shown to be a useful psychological construct, cross-cultural psychologists have recently also been interested in studying similarities and differences in self-concept across cultures, especially in Japan. But, one of the researchers' first discoveries was that the meaning of terms like *self* and *self-concept* was different in Japan from what it was in Europe and the U.S. As such, it was difficult to study it reliably.

A few years ago psychologists made great strides in their understanding of the constructs of self-concept across cultures and suggested that self-concepts differ fundamentally across cultures. More specifically, researchers Hazel Markus and Shinobu Kitayama (Markus and Kitayama 1991) and many other social scientists have come to believe that people in individualistic cultures have *independent* self-concepts. This means that the individual sees him- or herself as a distinct, separate, and autonomous entity. Others may be close, but they never penetrate the boundary between self and others. This independent self-concept is illustrated on the left side of Figure 2.7.

Figure 2.7

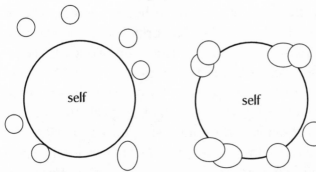

Independent Self-Concept   Interdependent Self-Concept

On the other hand, Markus and Kitayama wrote, and other social scientists concur, that people in supposedly collectivistic cultures such as Japan have an *interdependent* self-concept.[7] The interdependent self-concept is one in which the boundary between oneself and others is not as rigid as in the independent self-concept. Being autonomous, separate, and unique from others is not as important. Rather, this self-concept is based on the view that one is fundamentally and inextricably connected with others. Thus, perceptions of oneself are inevitably related to the existence of others in one's ingroup.

As you can imagine, there are many consequences for differences in behaviors between people with independent versus interdependent self-concepts. For example, people with independent self-concepts are supposed to be able to make decisions independently, with little or no reliance on the guidance or advice of others (see chapter 4 for more detail). People with interdependent self-concepts, however, are expected to pay special attention to the wishes and desires of those around them in making important decisions, because those others are a fundamental part of oneself. People with independent self-concepts are thought to perceive of themselves in terms of personal attributes, such as being friendly, outgoing, quiet, and the like. People with interdependent self-concepts are thought to perceive themselves in terms of the roles they play in society, such as father, mother, teacher, boss, and the like. People with independent self-concepts are thought to achieve things in life for themselves; people with interdependent self-concepts are thought to do so for the sake of others.

Social scientists have studied the differences between people with independent and interdependent self-concepts in many other ways as well. Most important for this discussion is the widely accepted notion that the Japanese have interdependent self-concepts while Americans and many other individualistic cultures have basically independent self-concepts. This stereotype, in fact, is in agreement with the stereotype discussed in the preceding section concerning collectivism and individualism.

The Evidence

Contemporary research in psychology provides no support for the stereotypic beliefs about the Japanese self-concept, however.[8] These studies have actually measured independent and interdependent self-concepts using valid and reliable measures. In the study briefly described above, for example, Carter and Dinnel (1997) measured independent and interdependent self-concepts in large samples of American and Japanese university students. When they analyzed the data, they found that the students in the two countries did not differ statistically on either type of self-concept, challenging the stereotype of Japanese interdependent self-construals.

Likewise, well-known author in the field of intercultural communication William Gudykunst and his colleagues administered a variety of scales measuring independent and interdependent self-concepts in Japanese, Korean, Australian, and American students (1992). Their data also revealed no statistically significant differences among Americans, Japanese, and Australians on either independent or interdependent self-concepts, once again challenging the stereotype of Japanese interdependent self-construals. Their data did show, however, that Koreans had significantly lower independent self-concept scores and higher interdependent self-concept scores, consistent with an Asian stereotype (Figure 2.8, page 52).

Some studies even report that Americans have more interdependent self-concepts than Japanese do, or that the Japanese have more independent self-concepts than do Americans, which is contrary to prevailing stereotypes. In one study by Ronald Kleinknecht, Dale Dinnel, and their colleagues, for instance, large samples of American and Japanese university students

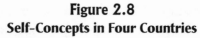

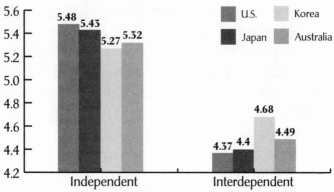

Figure 2.8
Self-Concepts in Four Countries

completed a scale measuring independent and inter-dependent self-concepts (Kleinknecht et al. 1997). The data revealed no difference between the two countries on independent self-concepts; the Americans, however, had significantly higher scores on interdependent self-concepts, directly contradicting the typical stereotype (see Figure 2.9 in the Appendix).

In yet another study, this one conducted by Min-Sun Kim and colleagues, participants in four groups—mainland United States, Hawaii, Japan, and Korea—completed two scales measuring independent and interdependent self-concepts (1996). Mainland Americans had the highest independent self-concept scores; Koreans had the lowest. The scores for the Japanese on this scale were similar to those for participants from Hawaii. In addition the participants from Japan had the lowest scores on interdependent self-concepts (Figure 2.10).

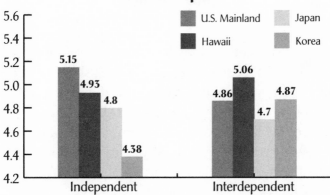

Figure 2.10
Self-Concepts

These studies, and others I have not discussed here, show rather convincingly that the stereotypic notions of scientists and laypersons about self-concepts and self-perceptions in Japan relative to countries such as Korea, Australia, and the United States are simply no longer true, especially for university students typically participating in social psychology research.[9] As with the research I described earlier, these studies have been conducted by Japanese and non-Japanese scientists, using different methodologies, over a long period of time. The reliability of their findings is, in my mind, without doubt or reproach. Clearly, this stereotype is simply not congruent with contemporary Japanese culture and the psychology of the younger generations.

Stereotype 3: Japanese Interpersonal Consciousness

Background

It is widely thought that Japanese people are highly conscious of others when making decisions and doing just about anything else. The degree to which people are aware of others in their lives and in their environment is known as *interpersonal consciousness*. It refers to an awareness of the existence of others and the degree to which this recognition affects or mediates one's behavior.

This perceived high degree of interpersonal consciousness is no doubt related to the stereotypes about Japanese collectivism and interdependent self-concepts. If the Japanese are collectivistic, the reasoning goes, and if they have interdependent self-concepts, then being relatively more conscious of others in normal life activities is a normal consequence because the existence of others is a fundamental aspect of their own sense of self and personality. Also, the supposed emphasis on collectivism suggests that Japanese individuals take into account the needs, wishes, desires, and goals of the group over their own individual needs and preferences.

In fact interpersonal consciousness *is* related to the notion of an interdependent self-concept as described in the preceding section. If the perceived Japanese collectivistic culture fosters an interdependent self-concept, then the Japanese self is fundamentally and profoundly intertwined with the existence of others. One cannot think, the reasoning goes, about oneself or about issues regarding the self independently of thinking about others. This construct is widely used by contemporary scientists in many social areas to explain cultural differences in behavior between Japan and other cultures.

The Evidence

To a large extent, however, this stereotype, too, is not supported by the data presented so far in this chapter. These data already clearly suggest that the notion of Japanese interpersonal consciousness may be more myth than reality.

Aside from the studies already reviewed, one study speaks directly to the notion of the degree to which Americans and Japanese emphasize social context when making decisions (which is a form of interpersonal consciousness). In this study, conducted jointly by an American and a Japanese researcher (Arikawa and Templer 1998), American and Japanese university students completed two scales. One scale measured collectivism, and the other measured consciousness concerning social context. When the researchers analyzed the data on the first scale, they found that the Americans had a slightly higher average score on collectivism than did the Japanese, but this difference was not statistically significant. The results are, however, consistent with many other studies and with those above addressing Stereotypes 1 and 2. When the researchers analyzed the social context scale, they again found that the Americans had a higher average score than did the Japanese, and this difference *was* statistically significant, indicating that the Americans, not the Japanese, had higher degrees of (at least this aspect of) interpersonal consciousness.

In another study Japanese social psychologist Yoshihisa Kashima and his colleagues administered a battery of psychological tests to university students in Australia, Japan, Korea, mainland United States, and Hawaii (Kashima et al. 1995). The tests included a scale that measured *kanjin shugi*, or the degree of interpersonal or relationship consciousness. The researchers believed that the Japanese and Koreans would have the highest scores on this scale, in congruence with the stereotype of Asian collectivism. When they analyzed the data, however, they found that mainland American women had the highest scores on this scale, followed by Australian women. Japanese women had the third to lowest scores, and Japanese men had the lowest (Figure 2.11).

Considered together with the research reviewed previously concerning collectivism and self-concepts, the studies reviewed here indicate quite convincingly that Japanese university students do not have high degrees of interpersonal or interrelationship consciousness when making decisions or engaging in other types of behaviors. This stereotype, also, appears to be more myth than reality.

Figure 2.11
Interpersonal Relationship Consciousness

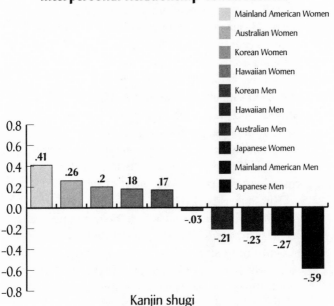

Kanjin shugi

Stereotype 4: Japanese Emotionality

Background

Over one hundred years ago, Lafcadio Hearn, whom I mentioned in chapter 1, spent the last fourteen years of his life in Japan and wrote several books about his newly adopted country. Throughout those books he marveled at how the Japanese people and culture were so different from those of Europe and the West. At one point in his book *Glimpses of Unfamiliar Japan* he wrote about the Japanese smile.

A Japanese can smile in the face of death, and usually does. But he then smiles for the same reason that he smiles at other times. There is neither defiance nor hypocrisy in the smile; nor is it to be confounded with the smile of sickly resignation which we are apt to associate with weakness of character. It is an elaborate and long cultivated etiquette. It is also a silent language. But any effort to interpret it according to Western notions of physiognomical expression would be just about as successful as an attempt to interpret Chinese ideographs by their real or fancied resemblance to shapes of familiar things....

The smile is taught like the bow, like the prostration.... But the smile is to be used upon all pleasant occasions, when speaking to a superior or to an equal, and even upon occasions which are not pleasant; it is part of deportment. The most agreeable face is the smiling face; and to present always the most agreeable face possible to parents, relatives, teachers, friends, wellwishers, is a rule of life.... Even though the heart is breaking, it is a social duty to smile bravely. ([1894] 1976, 658–59)

As I mentioned in chapter 1, Hearn, like so many people before and after him, saw the Japanese as humble, persevering people who, in the face of danger, threat, grief, and other disheartening emotions, manage to maintain a sense of dignity about themselves as they smile. He also saw the Japanese as having instituted politeness as a social rule and as having brought mannerisms and etiquette in social interaction to their highest standard.

What Hearn wrote about has been commented on by many other social scientists interested in the expressive behavior of the Japanese. These notions have contributed to a stereotype about Japanese emotionality that is commonly characterized by the notion of the "inscrutability" of the Japanese; that is, they never show their true emotions and often choose to smile to conceal their true feelings. Such notions have also contributed to the stereotype of the Japanese as emotionless robots. Westerners have also inferred the lack of variety and intensity in expressive behavior to be indicative of a lack of subjective emotional experience. These notions about Japanese emotions and expressive behaviors fit in well with the stereotypic notions about Japanese culture and society described in chapter 1, in both classical and contemporary portrayals.

The Evidence

These stereotypic notions were actually confirmed in a well-known psychology experiment conducted over thirty years ago by psychologists Paul Ekman and Wallace Friesen (Ekman 1972; Friesen 1972). They asked American and Japanese university students to come to a laboratory, where they watched films that were designed to make them feel disgusted, angry, sad, and even fearful.[10] During the first viewing the students watched the films individually, with no one else in the room. During this time their facial expressions were being videotaped. When their videotaped expressions were later analyzed, the researchers saw that the Americans and Japanese produced almost exactly the same expressions of disgust, anger, sadness, and fear at about the same times during the film. In a second part of the experiment, the same participants watched the films again in the presence of an older experimenter. This time the researchers found that the Americans generally showed the same negative expressions as in the first session. The Japanese students, however, almost invariably smiled during the times they felt negative emotions, even though they had revealed the negative emotions in the first viewing.

Ekman and Friesen interpreted the data by suggesting that the Japanese had a display rule that did not allow them to reveal their true feelings in the presence of the experimenter; in fact, they chose to hide their feelings with smiles, pretending as if everything was okay. The concept of cultural display rules was originally coined by Ekman and Friesen in 1969 and refers to rules learned throughout life that dictate the modification of expressive behavior depending on social circumstances. All people in all cultures and societies learn the rules of appropriate expression so that they may act as socialized agents within their own societies. The existence of Japanese cultural display rules, therefore, provides us with a mechanism that can explain expressive differences in public and private situations, *omote* and *ura* ("front" and "back"), *honne* and *tatemae* ("true feelings" and "outward appearances"), and the like.

Findings such as Ekman and Friesen's tended to reinforce the stereotypic view that the Japanese never show their true emotions, at least in public. That the Japanese students smiled despite what must have been quite intense, negative feelings is similar to what Hearn wrote in *Glimpses of Unfamiliar Japan* (see quote on page 58). When interpreted through Western eyes and cultural filters, this view has also led to negative attitudes and value characterizations of the Japanese, that they are less emotional, value feelings less, and are less trustworthy, sincere, and appropriate.

But these global, overarching stereotypes are probably not true today. The first matter to consider is that the data in Ekman and Friesen's study were collected in the late 1960s, a considerable time ago. Whether cultural trends and behaviors are the same today, after the extensive social and economic changes that have occurred in Japan during that time period, is highly questionable. I would doubt that the same findings would be obtained in a similar study today.[11]

Contemporary research has shown that Japanese people are highly emotional, that they value their and other people's emotions, and that interpersonal relationships depend on accurate, if not tacit, communication of emotions and feelings. These claims were supported in a study I conducted where American and Japanese university students rated the appropriateness of expressing seven different types of emotions in eight different social situations (Matsumoto 1990). If the Japanese conformed to the overall stereotype, the data would have indicated that they expressed emotions less frequently than Americans did in all social contexts and for all emotions. I found, however, that this was simply not the case. The Japanese did indeed express negative emotions less toward ingroup members—family, friends, work colleagues, and peers— than did the Americans. The Japanese also, however, expressed positive emotions *more* frequently than did the Americans toward these same groups. When we examined the data for outgroup relationships, the results were reversed; the Japanese expressed more negative emotions and fewer positive emotions toward outgroups than did the Americans (Table 2.1).

Table 2.1
Expression of Emotions

	With ingroups (family, friends, work colleagues, peers, etc.)	With outgroups (strangers, casual acquaintances, etc.)
Positive emotions	Japanese > Americans	Americans > Japanese
Negative emotions	Americans > Japanese	Japanese > Americans

Why does this rather complex pattern of findings emerge? There are, I believe, two factors that explain these findings. First, the Japanese learn to contextualize their behavior more than Americans do.[12] That is, the Japanese learn that different behaviors are appropriate in different contexts, depending on whom one is with, what is occurring, the setting, the target of the emotion, and the like. American display rules, on the other hand, call for less differentiation across contexts; individuals prefer to reveal their personalities, preferences, emotions, and styles across contexts. In short, Americans vary their behavior less according to context. For example, Americans would prefer to have the environment change to match their individual styles and preferences rather than to change their behavior. Japanese, on the other hand, prefer to accommodate to the contexts, which allows them to vary their behavior more.[13]

Understanding American and Western preferences for cross-context consistency allows us to easily understand how previous stereotypes about Japanese emotionality were created and fostered. When outsiders view Japanese emotions, oftentimes they are in situations or contexts in which the suppression of emotions is dictated by Japanese cultural display rules. But because Americans believe in cross-context consistency, they generalize this tendency to *all* contexts, inferring that Japanese people hide their emotions—or have no emotions—in general. The problem is compounded by the fact that many Japanese themselves contribute to this stereotypic attribution by claiming that they always suppress their true feelings.[14]

The second factor for this pattern of data is related to the meanings of specific emotions. We know from work in sociology, psychology, and anthropology that emotions have different social meanings. Some emotions, for example, help to create and maintain bonds among people. The shared joy of a group achievement or the shared sadness at the loss of a loved one in a family oftentimes brings people closer together. Other emotions, however, help to cut bonds or to differentiate among people. Anger, jealousy, frustration, and scorn can easily drive wedges between people, disrupting group harmony and cohesion.

When we put these two factors together—contextualization and the differential social meanings of emotions—we can easily understand the data. Japanese may amplify positive emotions and downplay negative emotions toward ingroups because these actions help them to create stronger bonds with these groups of individuals, fostering harmony and cohesion. On the other hand, they also amplify negative emotions and downplay positive ones to outsiders because these emotions help them to differentiate between their ingroups and outgroups. Such a pattern of data would not occur as much in the United States because there is greater need for consistency in individual behavior regardless of context.

In actuality such notions support the contention of Japanese collectivism, contradicting the evidence presented earlier in this chapter on that topic. There are two points that deserve mention here. Much of the evidence reviewed in Stereotype 1 contradicting Japanese collectivism was generally collected in the 1990s. The data collected in the display rule study described in this section, however, was collected in the 1980s, ten years earlier. While in the broader picture, ten years is not really a long time in terms of cultural changes, in the case of Japan, I would contend that one can witness considerable cultural changes during this time frame.

Second, the evolution of Japanese culture from collectivistic to noncollectivist need not occur across all domains of psychological behavior. It is entirely possible, for example, that attitudes and values, variables that are typically measured in questionnaires, may change while actual behaviors and expressions may be slower to change. If different domains of behavior change at a differential pace, this would explain why the data in Stereotype 1 and this stereotype appear contradictory.

Not only are traditional stereotypes about Japanese emotional expressions incomplete; contemporary psychological research on Japanese perceptions of others' emotions also points out that Japanese are very emotional. My colleagues and I have conducted a number of studies examining American and Japanese differences in emotional perception. These studies have a relatively simple methodology. Participants view different expressions, and for each one they tell us what emotion is being portrayed, how strongly it is being expressed on the outside (i.e., the display intensity), and how strongly the person is probably feeling it on the inside (i.e., the experience intensity) (e.g., see Matsumoto, Kasri, and Kooken 1999). When we showed American and Japanese university students pictures of neutral faces—that is, faces with no emotional content—there was no difference in their judgments about the pictures. Thus, we were confident that there was no difference between the American and Japanese bases for their ratings. When we showed them pictures of weak, moderately strong, and very strong expressions, however, the distinctions between the two groups were clear. In each instance, Japanese observers believed that the poser in the picture was feeling *more* emotion and at greater intensity than did the Americans. Thus, the Japanese participants *assumed* that more intense emotions were being felt by people than the Americans did, regardless of the actual intensity of the expression (Table 2.2).

Table 2.2
Reaction to Pictures Showing Emotions

Intensity of Expression	Differences in Perception of the Poser's Subjective Experience
Neutral	No differences between American and Japanese observers
Weak	Japanese observers saw more intense emotions than Americans did
Moderately Strong	"
Very Strong	"

The data from these studies argue convincingly that the global, overarching stereotype about Japanese inscrutability and their emotionlessness is not accurate, at least for the Japanese university student populations that were the participants in our many studies in this area. If anything, I believe the Japanese are highly emotional and value their own feelings and those of others above all else. Much of Japanese culture and society, in fact, is characterized by rituals and customs to preserve the sanctity and importance of human emotion, not downgrade it. I believe that the Japanese emphasis, not de-emphasis, on the importance of emotion can be seen in everyday discourse, in the logic underlying many Japanese cultural artifacts and rituals, in literature, media and film, and in historical events.[15] The reason many researchers in the past could not see the full range of Japanese emotions was probably because they had never studied the whole range across a wide variety of contexts. Furthermore, Westerners most likely interpreted the meaning and importance of emotion through their own cultural filters.

Stereotype 5: The Japanese Salaryman

Background

One reason Japan has become a major economic power since World War II is the well-known work ethic of the Japanese company employee. In Japan an employee of a company is typically called a "salaryman." This term generally calls forth a stereotypic image of an individual who has sacrificed his (usually male) life for the sake of the company. He spends long hours at the office, often working late into the night, and doesn't hesitate to come to work on the weekends, sacrificing personal and family time. He commutes hours every day to his job and works diligently and loyally, for the sake of the company and the Japanese economy as a whole. His social relationships are often with colleagues in the company, and he is often willing to move to different areas of Japan, and lately to the rest of the world, for the sake of the company.

Many non-Japanese have characterized Japanese salarymen as "samurai in suits," likening them to the bushido warrior class of the past and its associated set of values and norms. This concept became extremely popular throughout the 1970s and 1980s, partially as a way to explain Japan's economic recovery and boom. The salaryman became an image for literally millions of Japanese employees who were united in a single campaign not only for their own business and company but for national prosperity as well.

The image of the loyal salaryman became a stereotype; he was in many senses the backbone of the Japanese economy. Of course Japanese products excelled in quality in many areas of the world, but the Japanese salaryman and his work ethic were the heart and soul of Japan's development and progress. The focus on Japan's work ethic, on the salaryman's perseverance and fortitude, is undoubtedly a remnant from both classic and contemporary views of Japanese culture and society. Attitudes about and stereotypes of the Japanese salaryman are shared not only by Westerners but by the Japanese themselves.

The Evidence

Some evidence suggests that the stereotype of the salaryman is apropos today. For instance, a few recent surveys of Japanese workers seem to suggest that they are highly satisfied with their jobs. The EPA, for example, sampled 3,392 salarymen in 1995 and found that 62.1 percent of them reported that they were either "satisfied" or "fairly satisfied" with their current position. In a similar poll conducted by *Asahi Shimbun* in 1996, 66 percent of the respondents reported that they were satisfied.

A closer inspection of the data, however, suggests that all is not well among the so-called salarymen. For example, in the data reported by the EPA, there were two factors that were associated with differences in satisfaction—income and company size. The data indicated that people with larger incomes were more satisfied than were people with smaller incomes, suggesting that younger workers are generally less satisfied with their jobs than older workers, because younger workers generally have lower salaries. This is true for both men and women. Remember, the data presented in the first four stereotypes in this chapter were gathered from Japanese university students. Here, however, is evidence of dissatisfaction among relatively young Japanese workers, who have graduated from the universities and thus extend the previous findings beyond college life.

The EPA data also indicated that workers in larger companies were more dissatisfied than were workers in smaller companies. This finding is counterintuitive, because larger companies generally offer greater income, employment stability, and fringe benefits such as employment-related housing. Thus, the greater dissatisfaction among the younger employees is *not* simply a matter of money. This finding also goes against the preference of many Japanese salarymen in the past to work for larger, more stable companies.

Company size is also negatively related to perceptions about work. Individuals who were employed by larger companies often reported that "working is no more than a means to earn income" more than did individuals employed by smaller companies. This notion is also confirmed by the 1996 *Asahi Shimbun* study in which most Japanese workers reported that they considered their job basically as a source of income. A smaller percentage saw their jobs as their purpose in life. These data run contrary to the prevalent stereotype of the past, where larger companies offered individuals a lifetime career and were not simply viewed as a method of making money. These data also contradict the previous stereotype of the salaryman as a "worker bee," dedicating his life to benefit the company and the Japanese economy. In addition, these data run contrary to the responses of a similar group of individuals in the United States in the *Asahi Shimbun* report (Figure 2.12).

There have also been important shifts in employee attitudes toward work and effort. In the EPA study, while most of the Japanese respondents reported that they "try to do their best for their company," this large percentage was clearly carried by many of the older workers with higher incomes. In fact, closer inspection of the data indicated that employees in the 20–29 and 30–39 age groups were significantly less inclined to report that they try to do their best for the

Figure 2.12
How Employees View Their Jobs

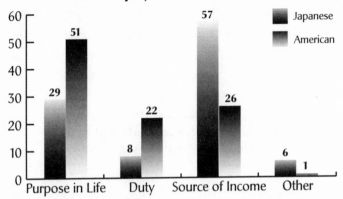

company. And employees of larger companies, and those with less income, reported less inclination to do their best. Clearly these data correlate with employee satisfaction as described above and run contrary to the worker bee stereotype of the salaryman.

One of the pillars of the Japanese human resources system is the pay-based-on-seniority system. That is, as employees age, their pay usually increases, oftentimes regardless of ability or merit. Yet, this pillar is gradually crumbling. In the EPA study a whopping 76.5 percent of the respondents indicated "companies should pay more attention to differences in individual ability in deciding salaries and promotions." The percentage of respondents agreeing with this statement was understandably lowest among men with the highest incomes. The results from the *Asahi Shimbun* survey were similar (see Figure 2.13 in the Appendix).

In fact a majority of employees clearly favor a merit system of wages, and their ranks have grown substantially since 1978 (52.4% in 1978 to 63% in 1995). The preference for a merit system is stronger among younger workers (but still is shared by more than half of workers in the 50–59 age group) (Figure 2.14).

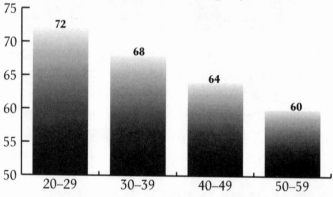

Figure 2.14
Age-Group Breakdown of Employees Favoring Merit-Based Wage System

These data suggest that current Japanese workers are not content to start at the bottom and spend their entire working life climbing their way up gradually, with no relationship between their pay and their abilities aside from their age. Consequently, there are growing numbers of employees who are increasingly dissatisfied with the way their efforts are rewarded in their companies, which is yet another contradiction to the stereotypic image of the Japanese salaryman (Figure 2.15).

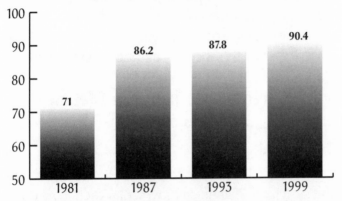

Figure 2.15
Employees Ambivalent toward
or Dissatisfied with Reward System

On top of this the EPA data clearly indicate that employees with higher educational degrees desire social status and promotion. Research has also shown that many of these same individuals, especially those who have received undergraduate and graduate degrees from American or European universities, feel that they deserve more frequent promotions and higher pay than others. These highly educated employees also add to a growing sentiment of change.

Collectively, the data in this section demonstrate rather convincingly that employee attitudes in Japan are quickly changing. In summary more Japanese employees view their jobs merely as a means of obtaining an income rather than as a career or their purpose in life. More Japanese individuals are rejecting the seniority-based system and prefer salary schedules and benefits that are based on achievement and ability. Taken altogether, the stereotype of the Japanese salaryman who is willing to sacrifice himself and his family, who is happy to be a worker bee for the sake of company and country, and who does not relish rewards based on individual achievements is more myth than reality, especially among younger workers.

Stereotype 6: Japanese Lifetime Employment

Background

One of the pillars of Japanese society in the past was the system of lifetime employment. When individuals joined a company, they were expected to stay with the company for their entire working lives. Both the company and the employee shared a reciprocal sense of duty and obligation. The company was obligated to provide for the employee for life, not only in terms of salary increases but also by providing opportunities for personal growth and expansion of duties and responsibilities commensurate with ability and the overall harmony and balance of the company. Employees reciprocated with their undying loyalty to the company; they were expected to stay with the company through good economic times and bad and to sacrifice their lives for the sake of the company (and for the national good).

This foundation of expected reciprocal obligation in Japanese society also had important ramifications for all other aspects of society, especially education.

Almost every mother in Japan strongly believed in the importance of an education. A good university degree, it was thought, would lead to employment in a reputable company, which would in turn become a lifetime commitment. Employees gave their entire lives to a company and expected the company to give them guaranteed employment in return. Lifetime employment meant stability, which, in turn, required a high standard of excellence from the educational system—from preschool all the way to university. Thus, many families put considerable pressure on their children to perform in school, even as early as preschool, so that they could later be accepted to and graduate from a good university and become employed by a reputable company. This belief is still prevalent today and is one of the reasons why high school students spend so much time, effort, and money preparing for university entrance exams. And this filters down to entrance exams for high school taken by junior high students, for junior high taken by elementary school students, and in some cases, even for elementary school taken by preschoolers. This social pressure undoubtedly led to the creation of such terms as *kyoiku mama* (education mama).

The social obligations incurred by the Japanese companies in the form of lifetime employment, and those incurred by the individual employees, are directly in line with the stereotypes of Japanese culture and society cultivated over the years. Obligation, commitment, loyalty, sense of duty, and sacrifice are exactly those values and attitudes that have characterized Japanese culture in both classic and contemporary works.

The Evidence

The harsh reality of the economic crises faced by Japan over the past decade, however, has resulted in an important change in these beliefs. Results from governmental EPA surveys in 1999, for example, indicated clearly that the number of companies that offer lifetime employment had dropped from 27.1 percent in 1990 to only 9.9 percent in 1999.[16] At the same time, companies abandoning lifetime employment increased from 36.4 percent to 45.3 percent during that same period. And the percentage of companies that were in limbo regarding lifetime employment and other personnel issues also rose from 25.4 percent to 38.3 percent.

As Japanese companies increasingly abandon lifetime employment, many are adopting a merit system in their labor management practices (reported in the EPA survey report of 1999). This type of system rewards abilities and achievements and no doubt reflects the demands of increased world competition on Japanese businesses and the changing attitudes of the contemporary Japanese worker.

These changes in Japanese companies have been accompanied by changes in the attitudes of Japanese employees. While most employees would certainly prefer to stay with the same company throughout their working life, a full 60.8 percent of the respondents from the EPA's 1995 survey indicated that they would change jobs if their work did not match their expectations or abilities. These data are complemented by the 1996 survey by *Asahi Shimbun* that indicated that a full 47 percent of the people surveyed believed they should change jobs if they were dissatisfied with the work. In fact, from 1987 to 1998, the number of people wishing to change jobs gradually and steadily increased, for both men and women (see Figure 2.16 in the Appendix).

While lifetime employment has greatly diminished in Japan, the number of part-time employees continues to rise for both men and women, according to the 1999 EPA survey. This trend no doubt reflects the answer to the problems many companies have experienced due to rising costs associated with hiring permanent lifetime employees (see Figure 2.17 in the Appendix).

According to figures released by the EPA in 1999, a full 19 percent of individuals 25 to 29 years of age hoped to become entrepreneurs rather than seek lifetime employment in a single company. Moreover, this figure was relatively stable at approximately 20 percent through age 54 for all individuals seeking a job change.

The recruitment of new employees in April, following March graduations, has also gradually declined over the years. In 1998, 88.7 percent of recruits were new graduates; the remainder were not. In five years the number of new graduate recruits in white-collar jobs is projected to drop to 80.6 percent, while the recruitment of older graduates and flexible recruitment (the recruitment of anyone at anytime) are projected to increase to over 19 percent. In some specialty fields, such as research and technical areas, the number of new graduate recruits projected is even lower, according to the same EPA survey in 1999.

These data suggest that the stereotype of guaranteed lifetime employment stability is more myth than reality in today's Japan. Today's employees believe in ability, achievement, and merit as the primary deciding factors influencing wage increases and promotion. They are increasingly unafraid to change jobs or to become entrepreneurs. There is no longer a guarantee of a good job in a stable company immediately after graduation, and even if one is lucky enough to get a job, there is no guarantee that the company will make a lifetime commitment or that the employee will voluntarily stay with the company for life. The belief in the link between a university education and lifetime employment is more myth than reality.[17]

The data presented in this section and the previous one speak clearly to the point that Japanese business culture, at least as represented in the minds, attitudes, values, and beliefs of the typical Japanese employee (especially but not limited to younger ones) is quite different from the stereotype about the Japanese worker held for years after the war. These differences have led to meaningful and important changes in many Japanese business practices, particularly in relation to personnel, human resources, and labor management. These alterations, in turn, affect everything from commitment and loyalty to recruitment, retention, and termination. Japanese business culture, like its mainstream societal culture, is going through a major transition.

Another important point about the data in these two sections is that this evidence suggests that the changes in Japanese cultural values held by university students clearly extend to the younger generations in the workforce. In other words, these data support the contention that the changes we are witnessing are not just a fad or a result of university life; they are, in fact, representative of the broader changes in culture and society that are occurring in Japan today.

Stereotype 7: The Japanese Marriage

Background

One of the pillars of Japanese society has undoubtedly been marriage. In traditional Japanese marriage, labor and responsibility were clearly divided between men and women. Men worked and were responsible for everything outside the home. The women managed the family finances, raised the children, and looked after all household affairs (and were typically the kyoiku mama, pushing their kids to complete their homework, participating in school activities for parents, enrolling their children in cram schools known as *juku*, and the like). The husband was lord of his castle, expecting and receiving obedience and conformity from wife and children. Quite frankly, husbands were masters, and wives devotedly supported their husbands.

This view of marriage and the separate roles for men and women are clearly rooted in classic conceptions of Japanese culture. The very structure and functioning of the Japanese household is firmly rooted in Confucian and other religious tenets concerning hierarchical relationships within the house. This very concept was so important to Japanese culture and society that Chie Nakane also linked it with the structure of vertical relationships in her thesis (1970). Therefore, marriage and household provide the final stereotype that I will address here about Japanese culture and society.

The Evidence

Research over the past few years demonstrates quite convincingly that fewer Japanese than ever agree with previous views of marriage and family life. From 1983 to 1995, for example, there was a sharp decrease in the percentage of men and women who agreed with the view that a wife should devotedly support her husband. There was also a decrease in the percentage of individuals surveyed who agreed with the less conservative view that the father works while the wife looks after the family. At the same time, there was an increase in the percentage of individuals who saw husbands and wives pursuing their own individual and independent lifestyles. More people also came to believe that husbands and wives should be good friends, and a small percentage of people in 1995 felt that husbands should defer to their wives (Figure 2.18).[18]

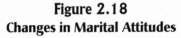

Figure 2.18
Changes in Marital Attitudes

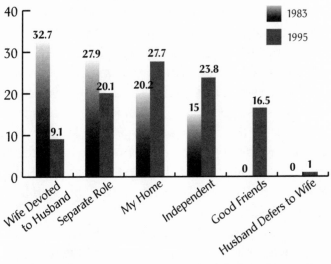

These changes are consonant with data from other surveys as well. According to *Asahi Shimbun's* survey in 1996, for example (compared with responses from 1994), more people disagreed that males should concentrate on their jobs while females should do their best in housekeeping and child care (52% in 1996 versus 36% in 1994). And in its 1997 survey, *Asahi Shimbun* asked respondents whether they viewed husbands and wives as one flesh or as independent people. Although 29 percent saw married couples as one flesh, an overwhelming 69 percent saw married couples as two independent people.

Also contributing to this trend is the finding in some surveys that the most dissatisfied married couples are those who live with the husband's mother, which is a traditional arrangement in Japanese families. This finding is true for both husbands and wives.

While marriage was seen as the ultimate goal for women in the past, increasing numbers of women today approve of a single lifestyle. In the 1997 EPA survey, in fact, 55 percent of the women polled approved of a single lifestyle. These data agree with other vital statistics reported by the Japanese government that indicate that women are marrying at later ages and having children later as well. They also have greater life expectancies than in the past and are probably asking questions about how they want to spend their longer lives.

Indeed, greater numbers of people than ever before have come to the conclusion that human happiness is not only to be found in marriage. And following quite naturally from this conclusion, increasing numbers of Japanese individuals are finding it appropriate to get divorces when things don't go well in their marriage (Figure 2.19).

Not only is divorce on the rise among younger couples; greater numbers of older married couples are also getting divorced, coming to the realization that nothing requires the couple to stay together after the children are raised. Moreover, most Japanese individuals surveyed believed that this trend toward divorce among older couples would increase (69% of all individuals surveyed).

Figure 2.19
Approval of Divorce

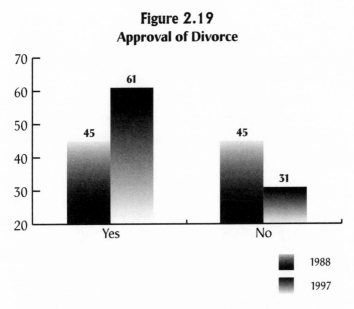

These data clearly indicate that the nature of the Japanese marriage has changed dramatically over the past decade. Furthermore, these changes are likely to continue into the near future. The husband-as-master and wife-devoted-to-husband style of marriage is a relic of the past. In fact in contemporary Japanese culture, one or even two divorces are really "no big deal." The term *batsu ichi*, translated literally as "one strike," has come to refer to people who have gotten divorced once, but they no longer have to live with the stigma of having done so. Moreover, many individuals in Japan do not mind and even prefer marrying someone who is batsu ichi, reasoning that he or she has experience with marriage and has supposedly grown from the experience. This is clearly contradictory to the classic and stereotypic views of marriage that in many ways formed the basis for much of Japanese culture. Thus, another stereotype is debunked.

Changes in the nature and function of marriage in any society, not only Japan's, have fundamental and profound implications regarding changes in all other aspects of culture and society, from education to child rearing and from business to dealing with old age. We will discuss some of these implications later in this book.

Conclusion

In this chapter I have provided evidence to suggest that previous classic and stereotypic views of seven aspects of Japanese culture and society are no longer true. These included aspects of Japanese character and personality: collectivism, self-concept, interpersonal consciousness, and emotionality. We also discussed changes in the attitudes and beliefs about the Japanese salaryman, lifetime employment, and Japanese marriage. Collectively, they paint a picture of contemporary Japan that does not conform to the stereotypic notions that previous *and* current works on Japanese culture conform to. To my way of thinking, many views of present-day Japanese culture are more myth than reality.

Of course, not all is changed in Japan, and one can still find many Japanese whose lives and lifestyles do indeed conform to our classic conceptualizations of Japanese culture. Because much of the research reported in this chapter has involved Japanese individuals in major cities like Tokyo and Osaka (and in other areas as well), it is entirely possible that much of what is reported here is limited to major urban areas and that life in less urban areas is more reflective of the stereotypic views of Japanese culture. I don't doubt that this is the case.

I am not arguing for an either-or case about the Japanese culture. What I am saying is that the amount of change in contemporary Japanese culture and society is sufficient to raise serious questions about the validity of previous stereotypic views of Japanese culture, especially those that purport a unicultural, homogeneous view of the culture and *all* of its people. While changes in seven areas of life are surely not comprehensive, I contend that they are representative of widespread changes in many other aspects of Japanese society today.

Textnotes

1 In actuality most of the data for *Culture's Consequences* (1980; 1984) were collected in the 1960s.

2 Detailed reviews of this literature can be found in Matsumoto 1999b; Takano and Osaka 1997; and Takano and Osaka 1999. Even Hofstede's data ranked Japan (relatively more collectivistic than the U.S.) in the middle of all countries surveyed on the individualism-collectivism scale.

3 See also the work by Nakane described in chapter 1 on the importance of the notion of ie in Japanese culture.

4 I do not believe, however, that these data argue against Nakane's concept of the importance of ie in Japanese society. On the contrary, I believe the notion of its importance is quite accurate and that changes in mainstream Japanese society and culture as a whole are probably related to changes in the fundamental nature of relationships within Japanese homes.

5 The data from this study may also indicate that Japanese collectivistic behaviors may exist only within a collectivistic system that incorporates moral sanctions and monitoring. That is, when the sanctions and monitoring are removed, the collectivistic nature of behavior disappears. The extent that this may be true is also evidence of changes in Japanese culture.

6 See Nakane's comments reported in chapter 1 on this issue.

7 I say *supposedly* here because I believe research on this issue says otherwise, as described earlier in this chapter. Indeed, the link between individualism-collectivism and independent-interdependent self-construals was essential to Markus and Kitayama's (1991) theory; they claimed that individualistic cultures foster an independent self-construal, while collectivistic cultures foster an interdependent self-construal.

8 Markus and Kitayama (1991) claim that there is substantial support for their argument that the Japanese have an interdependent self-construal. The research they cite to support their contention, however, never measured self-construals directly. Rather, it measured differences in a variety of psychological constructs and inferred the existence of self-construal differences to account for the observed differences in the other psychological variables. But the

evidence clearly does not support the view that such differences are rooted in differences in self-concept.

9 This really poses a problem for researchers who report differences between Americans and Japanese on other behaviors, because it is almost impossible to account for those differences by using cultural differences in self-construals when those differences don't actually exist in the first place.

10 The power of these films to elicit negative emotions was considerable, as they included scenes of amputations, sinus surgery, childbirth with forceps, and an aboriginal puberty rite with a rock.

11 By this comment, I do not mean to diminish the importance of Ekman and Friesen's study at the time it was conducted, or its findings. Indeed, their study remains a classic in the field of emotion research.

12 The acute reader may notice an apparent contradiction between the thesis in this passage and my review of the previous stereotype regarding Japanese interpersonal consciousness. On one hand, I suggest here that the Japanese consider context important and learn to contextualize their behaviors much more than the average American does. On the other hand, I described in the previous section how Japanese interpersonal consciousness is not necessarily greater than what would be expected in the United States. The apparent contradiction comes from the suggestion that the focus on contextualization is related to interpersonal consciousness. While the two concepts may be and often are linked, I believe that it is theoretically and pragmatically possible, however, to separate the two. Interpersonal consciousness as I have defined it here refers to the degree to which people recognize and are aware of others in their environment. Context, as used here, on the other hand, refers to a broader range of parameters of the environment, including time, place, setting, and situation as well as

others. It is entirely possible, therefore, that behavior be highly contextualized in the broader sense of the term *context* while interpersonal consciousness—the degree to which the awareness of others may affect behavior—is diminishing.

13 A simple illustration of this difference can be seen in everyday life. Say, fwor instance, that some obstacles are between you and your intended destination. Americans would be more likely to take the straight path, moving inanimate objects to get to their goal. Japanese, however, would be more likely to simply go around the objects. That is, for Americans, the context assimilates to their behaviors; Japanese people accommodate to context.

14 In actuality, what I think is occurring is that the Japanese do suppress their feelings and expressions in *some* contexts, but not all; and, as the data indicate, they probably exaggerate their expressions and feelings in some contexts. I think they extrapolate their suppression of feelings in some contexts to a stereotypic view of themselves, partly because it is noble and partly because those situations are often most stressful for them and therefore remain in their consciousness longer. Behavior can also change, at least superficially, while values and attitudes—and feelings—remain the same, as in the "cultural chameleon."

15 Japanese concepts such as perseverance, for example, refer to the control of emotion. Institutionalized politeness is a method for preventing offense and negative emotion. Compassion and honor have been themes for dramas and novels for centuries, highlighting the importance of emotion. In short, while the Japanese are encouraged to hide their emotions in some contexts, they are socialized to have a rich emotional life.

16 The EPA report cites the Ministry of Labor's "Survey on Employment Management" as the source of these figures.

[17] This is not to argue, however, that education is not important. In fact education may be crucial for people to gain the
skills to propel the graduate into merit-driven companies
or to launch entrepreneurial enterprises. The belief in the
importance of education in the future is probably evidenced
by the increasing number of students enrolled in colleges
and universities in Japan today despite the fact that the
absolute number of university-age individuals in the population is decreasing. What I argue for here is that the belief
in the *link* between education and lifetime employment is
more myth than reality.

[18] These data are reported in the EPA's 1995 report on the
National Survey on Lifestyle Preferences.

3

Why Did Japanese Culture Change?

So far, we have seen strong evidence to suggest that Japanese culture is in transition. The data from social psychology studies and national surveys speak for themselves, but they have also been confirmed by everyday life experiences living, working, and playing in Japan.

In this chapter I explore some of the reasons I think Japanese culture and society are undergoing such drastic changes. My analysis uses constructs and notions that are true not only for Japan, but are generally applicable to understanding cultural change and evolution in all parts of the world. Indeed, Japan is not alone in experiencing cultural change; what is special about the Japanese case, though, is the unique way in which the change is occurring in relation to previous stereotypic notions of the culture, and the apparent effects these shifts are having on social etiquette and morality at the start of this millennium. Before giving the reasons I think Japanese culture is evolving, let me first explain what I mean by the word *culture*, because this definition is integral to an understanding of how culture changes over time.

Understanding What Culture Is and Is Not

Common Usages of the Word *Culture*

First, let's examine how we use the word *culture* in our everyday language.[1] When we think of the word *culture*, we often think of nationality, race, or ethnicity. When we speak of culture, we talk about Japanese culture, American culture, French culture, and so on. This usage essentially equates nationality, race, or ethnicity with culture, and they are often used interchangeably. But, in my mind, culture is not nationality; it is not the citizenship on your passport. It is much more than that.

Culture as an Abstraction

Culture cannot be seen or felt or heard or tasted. What is concrete and observable to us is not culture per se but the differences in human behavior we see in actions, thoughts, rituals, traditions, and the like. We see *manifestations* of culture, but we never see culture itself. For example, look at the cultural differences in greeting behaviors. In many Western cultures, we learn to shake hands when we greet others, and hand-shaking has become ritualistic and automatic for many of us. People of other cultures, however, have different ways of greeting people. People of some cultures, for example, greet each other with a slight bow of the head. Some cultures enhance this bow with hands together in front as in prayer. Some cultures, like that of Japan, instruct their members to bow from the waist with the face lowered out of sight. Still other cultures engage in only an "eyebrow flash," the raising and lowering of the eyebrows. We can witness these actions, and many other behavioral manifestations of culture, but we never see culture itself. Instead, we infer that a cultural difference underlies these various behaviors and that because the behaviors are different, the culture must be different. Culture, then, is used as an explanatory concept to describe the reason behind the differences in behaviors that we see.

In this sense culture is an abstract concept. We invoke the concept of culture to describe similarities and differences among individuals within a group. In other words we use the concept of culture as an explanatory construct to help us understand and categorize within-group similarities and between-group differences. It is a theoretical or conceptual entity that helps us understand why we do the things we do and explains why different groups of people do things their own way. As an abstract concept, then, culture is very much a label.

The Cyclical and Dynamic Nature of Culture

But like many labels, culture has a life of its own. Just as similarities within and differences between groups give rise to what we know as culture as an abstract concept, that abstract concept feeds back on those behaviors, reinforcing our understanding of those similarities and differences. Culture, in whatever way we come to know it, helps to reinforce, promulgate, and strengthen the behavioral similarities and differences that produced it in the first place, producing a cycle of reciprocity between actual behaviors and our theoretical understanding of them as culture.

This reciprocal relationship helps explain why we are taught to do many things simply because *that is the way they have always been done and it is how they should be done*. Learning to eat a certain way, with a certain etiquette, with certain foods, with certain utensils, in a certain order, simply because "that's the way things are done" is just one of many examples of how the abstract concept of culture drives behavior. It is in this fashion that culture and the actual behaviors culture describes share an intimate relationship. While it may appear that culture is an abstract theoretical concept that "sits" above people and mysteriously influences our behavior, that is not the case. As an explanatory concept that people have created, culture shares a close relationship with behaviors. Thus, culture is a summative label for behaviors, while at the same time it influences and affects behaviors.

For this reason, changes in behaviors will necessarily bring about changes in culture. Because culture is a concept we produce to help us explain actual behaviors, a discrepancy between behavior and culture produces tension in this relationship that often leads to a change in culture. Therefore, as your behaviors change during the course of your life, however slightly, these changes may be related to changes in culture within yourself and across people of the same generation. Differences in behaviors between younger and older generations surely signal differences in the underlying culture of these two groups and contribute to the generation gap.

There is always some degree of discrepancy between the behaviors mandated by culture and the abstract concept of culture. That is, there is never a one-to-one correspondence between the behaviors mandated by an underlying culture and the actual behaviors that occur. There will always be some degree of discrepancy, however small, between the two, despite their close and intimate relationship. Thus, there is always a dynamic tension in this relationship. In this sense, even as an abstract concept or principle, culture is never a static entity. It is dynamic and changing, existing within a tensive relationship with the actual behaviors it is supposed to explain and predict. In fact, the degree of tension between culture as an underlying construct and the behaviors that it mandates may be an important aspect of culture itself.

Definition of Culture

To me culture is *an organized system of rules shared by a group of people and transmitted from one generation to the next*. It is the attitudes, values, beliefs, opinions, norms, customs, heritage, traditions, and behaviors that a group shares and that are communicated from generation to generation.

Applying this definition to Japan suggests that what is important about Japanese culture is not necessarily the fact that one is born and raised there[2]; it is, instead, the fact that Japanese people share, to some degree, an organized system of rules that govern their behaviors, actions, and so forth, and it is that which is communicated from one generation to the next. This is true, in fact, for all cultures.[3]

There is not necessarily a one-to-one correspondence between culture and nationality. Certainly, there is some kind of relationship between Japan and what we know as Japanese culture, just as there is a relationship between the United States and what we know as American culture. It is also true, though, that there are many degrees of individual differences in culture. That is, different people hold the values and attitudes of the mainstream culture to different degrees. So, just as we know people who are very "traditionally" Japanese, we also know Japanese people who are not.

Likewise, there is not a one-to-one correspondence between culture and race or ethnicity. In fact, close examination of the scholarly literature on race in biology, physical anthropology, and other disciplines indicates clearly that there are really no biological or genetic markers that reliably distinguish among groups of people. Theories (and evidence supporting those theories) concerning the origins of supposed races are also problematic and are fraught with difficulties. Moreover, the concept of race is different across different languages and cultures. Thus, the concept of race is not as stable as people assume it to be. Therefore, culture is not necessarily race, nationality, or ethnicity. It is a functional, sociopsychological construct that we all share. It is not biological or genetic; it is learned and it is environmental.[4]

On the other hand, there are groups of people who can probably be characterized as cultural groups according to the definition I offered earlier, but who are not usually considered cultures; for example, disabled individuals or people of different sexual orientations. What gives these groups their flavor and importance is their culture, defined as the sociopsychological organizational system of rules they all share.

Differences in Culture within Countries

Because culture exists in groups smaller than a nation and because there are always some members of any cultural population who do not hold the views, attitudes, opinions, and values of the larger, mainstream culture, there is always some degree of tension or conflict among the groups. Harry Triandis (1994; 1995), one of the leading cross-cultural psychologists, has reported that as many as 30 percent of the individuals in any cultural group do not necessarily conform to the mainstream values of the larger group. Thus, for example, in even the most individualistic cultures he has studied, around 30 percent of the people in those cultures actually hold collectivistic values. The same is true of collectivistic cultures. The findings from the studies I have conducted, reported in chapter 2—which revealed that around 70 percent of the younger generation were individualistic while 30 percent were not, and vice versa for the older working sample—are clearly commensurate with Triandis' thesis.

The United States offers an excellent example of the complexity of national culture. Many ethnic groups in the U.S. actually claim more traditional values of their homeland than do the members of their original countries. That is, Japanese Americans, Chinese Americans, Korean Americans, and Filipino Americans are often more traditionally Japanese, Chinese, Korean, and Filipino than people in their native countries. In one study we conducted, for example, we examined collectivistic values among Koreans in South Korea, third-generation Korean Americans, and non-Asian Americans (Lee 1995). We projected that the level of collectivism would order itself in this manner: Koreans > Korean Americans > non-Asian Americans; in reality the Korean Americans were the most collectivistic, more collectivistic than Koreans in Korea. Other scholars writing about immigrant Asian ethnic groups, such as Ronald Takaki of the University of California Berkeley, have also come to the same conclusion (see, for example, his *Strangers from a Different Shore*, 1989). So, we must realize that there is great diversity with regard to culture, even within national cultures.

Factors that Affect Culture

Because of these cultural dynamics, it is relatively easy to understand why any culture, not just Japanese, is a fluid, dynamic, ever-changing entity. Because culture is a summation of ways of living, it follows that if a people's ways of living change across time, their culture will change. I believe we see the results of this phenomenon at work all around the world today.

For this discussion, let me focus on two of the myriad of important factors I believe affect culture: population density and availability of resources. The particular combination of these two factors easily affects ways of life that are necessary for survival and that, in turn, affect (and are affected by) culture. Consider, for example, a possible classification scheme based on these two factors in relation to one dimension of culture—individualism/collectivism (see Table 3.1, page 100).

In a situation in which large numbers of people live in a relatively confined space (i.e., high population density) and where the availability of the resources necessary for living is low (such as low income, low degree of arable land for farming, etc.),[5] conditions necessitate considerable degrees of inter- and intra-group harmony, cooperation, and cohesion in order for individuals to survive. Indeed, individuals would find it difficult to survive alone, and survival itself would depend in large part on the ability of individuals to band together in sizable groups to pool resources, divide tasks, and share resources in order to live. These are some of the classic characteristics of collectivism and certainly are commensurate with previous conceptualizations of Japanese culture. I call this "traditional" collectivism.

Table 3.1
Two Factors Affecting Culture

| | | Population Density | | |
		High		Low
Resource Availability	High	"IC duality"	"Complex" individualism	"Traditional" individualism
	Low	"Traditional" collectivism		"Simple" collectivism

On the other hand, consider the context in which small numbers of people live in wide-open spaces with abundant resources for living (i.e., low population density), such as the American West in the 1800s or even the American Midwest today. Such people feel less compelled to work together, cooperate, collaborate; in other words, be collectivistic. They will instead be self-sufficient and relatively autonomous, which are the hallmarks of what I call "traditional" individualism.

In the case where population density is low and where resource availability is also low, collectivism is necessary in order to pool resources to survive. This pooling, however, occurs within relatively small groups of people or communities, with simpler social structures than societies with a high population density. This case may be exemplified by cultural groups in parts of Africa, Asia, or South America who are essentially isolated from urbanized or developed communities, but who lack the resources to survive without each other's help. For comparison purposes, I call this cultural typology "simple" collectivism.

The fourth typology in this table is a unique and fascinating case. I believe that the characteristics of the culture of people who live in areas of high population density and high resource availability depend on the cultural milieu of their history. Here things get a bit complicated. If a culture that is traditionally collectivistic, with high population density and low resource availability, gains resources to live, then I believe their culture has the potential for becoming more individualistic as their need to cooperate lessens. Should such a situation occur across generations, one potential outcome is that younger generations will develop a cultural orientation that is different (i.e., more individualistic) from their predecessors'. I label this situation "IC duality," where individualism (I) and collectivism (C) co-exist in different segments of the population.[6] This is exactly what I believe has happened in Japan (IC duality will be taken up in more detail below).

If, however, a culture that is traditionally individualistic, with low population density and high resource availability, experiences an increase in population density, I believe the people retain their basic individualism but that it is manifested in more complex ways because of more complex stratifications in society. I call this "complex" individualism. The difference in individualism in America, for example, between a rural town in the Midwest (traditional individualism) and the individualism exhibited in New York City or Los Angeles (complex individualism) would exemplify this evolution.

Surely there are many other factors that affect culture, including economic, political, geographic, climatic, and historical determiners. And there are many ways of understanding the influence of such factors on cultural dimensions other than the individualism and collectivism dimension. My main point here is that trends that affect the way of life of a people over a considerable length of time have the potential to change culture, because culture is the summation of the rules and systems of living. I believe that population density and resource availability are especially germane, however, to understanding the changes in Japanese culture over the past half century.

The thesis I wish to develop is that much of the confusion and conflict that currently exist in Japanese society results from the combination of at least two factors: a growing culture of individuality, especially among the younger generations, within a previously predominantly collectivistic society, and the perception of a lack of morality and social etiquette in today's youth. First I will describe the dramatic change in Japanese culture over the past fifty years, then the growth of individuality within Japan, and finally, the changing moral values in society.

Japanese Cultural Change

Cultural change occurs all over the world and for many different reasons. Refugees, asylum seekers, and immigrants to new lands, for example, often learn new cultural values as they assimilate. Countries invaded during wars are often forced to learn new cultures. Countries that receive large numbers of immigrants from one or more countries are exposed to their material goods and psychocultural artifacts—music, popular culture, and the like—often resulting in cultural change. And countries and cultures like Japan, which have undergone major changes in the fifty-some years since World War II, have experienced major social and cultural changes.

Japan is certainly not an anomaly in the sense that cultural change has been occurring. In fact all cultures of the world are constantly evolving because of changing environmental conditions. What is striking in the Japanese case, however, is the *speed* of transformation of cultural values from one end of the spectrum to the other.

To be sure, Japan was probably very collectivistic in the past, as we discussed in chapter 1. At the end of World War II, this collective consciousness was called to arms. The joint efforts of the entire country were necessary to rebuild the nation from the ruins in which it lay after the war. In addition Japanese pride required a strong and united front against the American occupation forces, who appeared to want to have their way with Japanese society and culture. Thus, Japan set out on a mission to rebuild and transform its economy into a power to be reckoned with, which of course also increased dramatically the availability of resources for its people.

The transformation from the end of the war until the present has been a miracle. The Japanese government's plan from 1961 to 1970, for example, called for the national income to be doubled by 1970 and for spectacular growth in a number of industrial sectors. History has proven that this ambitious plan was not a fantasy. Japan's average growth rate per year between 1946 and 1956 was 10.6 percent (compared with 4.3 percent in France). From 1957 to 1959, it was 9.2 percent, and from 1959 on it remained relatively high. In comparison, Japan's annual growth rate in the first half of the century was 4 percent.

Along with this rate of economic growth was concomitant growth in personal income. After the war the annual income for many individuals in Japan was $200–$300; by the 1960s it had risen to an astonishing average of $8,810 (in current income figures). Today, annual income is many times more than that. In addition personal investing compounded personal income. Many individuals made large amounts of money in the Tokyo stock exchange in the 1960s, but since that time more people have turned to deposit accounts and savings for their personal investments. The amount of savings per individual in Japan relative to the rest of the world has been well documented, with estimates as high as an average of 30 percent of expendable income. Higher incomes have meant increased spending for convenience goods, foods, and luxury items.

Today, as the world's second largest economy, Japan is one of the strongest nations in the world financially. And this transformation has had an enormous impact on the psychology of its people. Japanese individuals have more money and more items to make their lives more comfortable than ever before.

Thus, according to the analysis described above, the Japanese have had a substantial increase in the amount of resources available to them. And this is especially true when compared with the resources available to the Japanese people just one generation ago. The degree of increase in resource availability from one generation to the next cannot be denied.

At the same time, changes have occurred in population density. Although the actual amount of arable land in Japan has not changed appreciably, the birthrate, while climbing immediately after the war, has been declining ever since and is today at its lowest point since the war (Figure 3.1, page 106). Thus, there is a real decrease in the absolute numbers of people being added to the Japanese society.[7]

Figure 3.1
Japan's Birthrate since World War II

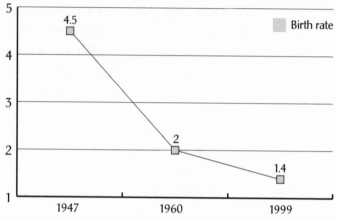

In addition, the introduction of personal convenience technologies, such as the Walkman stereo, cellular phones, and personal computers, have in my mind created an additional *psychological* distance between people. For instance, when people talk to their friends or acquaintances on the cell phone while on the train, they create a psychological distance between themselves and all the people around them. It is as if they don't exist. The same is true when people listen to their stereo headphones or stay at home and communicate with others almost exclusively by e-mail. A child listening to his or her Walkman in the family car on a drive somewhere has created psychological space between him- or herself and the rest of the family. Thus, technological advances and the declining birthrate have led to a *functional* decline in population density.[8]

According to the analysis described earlier, what has happened in the Japanese society is a functional decline in population density coupled with increased resource availability. These two facts lead to an inevitable decrease in collectivistic behaviors, values, and group consciousness, and an increase in individuality, uniqueness, and separateness. With greater resource availability, Japanese individuals no longer need to rely on each other for their survival, thus weakening collectivism and group consciousness considerably. In their place have risen individual effort and self-sufficiency. Individuality and uniqueness have come to overshadow more traditional collectivistic ways of thinking. This is why we observe the results I have reported in study after study on Japanese culture in social psychology and in surveys conducted in Japan by different agencies, as we discussed in chapter 2. In short, I believe Japan has moved from traditional collectivism to IC duality (refer back to Table 3.1 on page 100).[9]

Still, it is important not to lose sight of the fact that these changes are superimposed on a base of collectivism. As I mentioned earlier, a tensive relationship exists between culture and behavior, because not everyone conforms to the mainstream or predominant cultural mores. In the past this degree of tension within the Japanese culture was probably insufficient to make much of a difference to society at large. In addition, social rules and sanctions existed to deal with such divergences of culture and behavior (e.g., the socialization process within companies as described by Chie Nakane 1970). In Pertti J. Pelto's (1968) terminology, Japan was rather "tight"—homogeneous and monocultural. These characteristics were associated with an apparent peace and stability.

Yet, with the changes in ways of life and behavior in the past fifty years, the divergence between the older, stereotypic views of culture and actual real-life ways of living has grown, resulting in greater tension within society. As the divergence increases, social rules and sanctions for dealing with such divergent behavior no longer work. I believe it is this cultural tension that is contributing to much of the data we examined in the second half of chapter 1.

I leave this section of the chapter with a final thought about cultural change in Japanese history. Evidence for the fluidity of Japanese culture across different periods of history is strong and growing. Some historians believe, for example, that the Japanese culture was very open to the outside world and, by the way, individualistic from 1400 to 1600. During this time trade and relations were conducted with many other countries, and the nature of the psychology of the Japanese during this period of history was centered more on uniqueness and individuality than has been the case in recent history. The century of the Warring Period (Sengoku Jidai) and the closing of Japan and the beginning of the Tokugawa Period, however, had an enormous impact on the culture and psychology of the Japanese people as individuals. These social and political changes had large repercussions, which helped to divert the Japanese psyche back to the more traditional, conservative outlook of collectivism. With the rise of individuality, uniqueness, and separateness over the last fifty years, however, we now see another swing in the pendulum of culture. The changes are perhaps more rapid now than at previous points in history because of the technological and economic innovations that enable changes in culture to occur more rapidly now than in the past. Thus, Japanese culture has swung widely throughout history, and these swings are only natural when culture is seen as a sociopsychological construct that varies according to a number of external factors.

Changing Moral Values in Japanese Society

While the previous section discussed how the Japanese culture has changed from one of traditional collectivism to IC duality, another factor I believe has contributed to the growing state of confusion and unrest in contemporary Japanese society has to do with changes in moral values and social behavior during this same time period. An increase in the cultural values of individualism and separateness in and of itself is not necessarily a cause for concern in contemporary Japanese society, or in any society. What has been a cause for concern, however, is the perception that many of the younger generations today, who seemingly hold views of newfound cultural individuality, are also considered to lack the morality or ethics that would make them decent citizens.

This perception is well noted by surveys of Japanese individuals conducted by the Japanese government. In the EPA's 1995 survey, for instance, which involved a random sampling of 4,400 Japanese men and women between the ages of 20 and 59 (3,392 valid responses), individuals at all age ranges felt that children and juveniles in general lacked basic moral skills and social etiquette (see Figure 3.2 in the Appendix).

While some people believe that only the older generations lament the changes in moral virtues in the younger generations, what is striking about these data is that people ranging in age from 20 to 59 believe there is a problem in morals and social etiquette. Thus, the cry for social discipline is not a generational issue; it is a social issue that permeates all levels of society.

When the surveyed individuals were asked to identify the specific aspects of behavior they thought were lacking in youth today, most people chose as follows: (1) perseverance, (2) good manners, (3) responsibility, and (4) tolerance and generosity of spirit. In addition public-mindedness and economy were also mentioned by a large number of those surveyed (Figure 3.3, page 111, lists the top six answers given by respondents).

Figure 3.3
Behaviors Youth Are Lacking

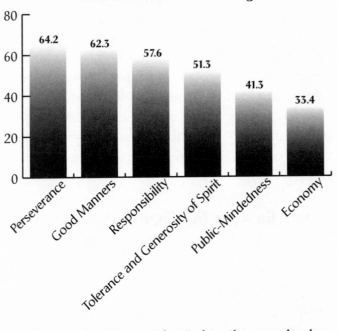

These concerns are identical to the moral values and virtues espoused by Japanese and non-Japanese alike in previous stereotypic conceptualizations of Japan. Perseverance, good manners, responsibility, tolerance, and public-mindedness read as if they come from Inazo Nitobe's *Bushido* or Ruth Benedict's *The Chrysanthemum and the Sword*. Thus, the changes in moral virtues perceived by many of the current population in Japan speak to the heart and soul of the Japanese culture and character as recognized for centuries.

These changes in moral virtues and social behavior compound the difficulties brought about by the

changing cultural values described earlier in this chapter. Some may say that changing morality is a product
of changing culture; others may advocate the opposite. To me, it doesn't matter which produces which;
the fact of the matter is that they both occur and are
perceived simultaneously in contemporary Japanese
culture, and for that reason, it is the association between a growing culture of individuality and the perception of lack of morality and social etiquette that is
a cause of confusion and conflict in Japanese society
today.

Some Reasons for Changing Morals and Social Behavior in Japan

There are undoubtedly many factors that contribute
to the changing morality in Japan, just as there are
multiple factors that cause cultural change in any society. In this section, I examine two main factors:
parenting and child-rearing practices, and social
causes.

Before delving into this subject in more detail, however, it is important to note that I recognize that some
Japanese readers may perceive that I am blaming them
for the decline in morality. I intend no such blame.
Rather, I attempt to identify and explain the factors I
believe are contributing to these changes, and parents, for example, are partially responsible for those
changes. Responsibility, however, is different from
blame; the latter is negative, which I do not intend to

be. Rather, I am attempting to describe the changes in morality and the public's perceptions of them in as objective a manner as possible, without placing my own value judgments on them. (I will, however, in the last chapter offer personal comments about the new moral values and their future.)

Child Rearing and Parenting: The Impact of an Unbalanced Emphasis on Education

In my view one of the major contributing factors to the changes in social behavior that Japan has witnessed in recent years is related to child-rearing and parenting practices, that is, what goes on in the home. One of the largest influences on child-rearing practices in contemporary Japan has been the almost exclusive emphasis on education and the interesting and peculiar family dynamics this emphasis has created in many Japanese families.

As we discussed in Stereotype 6 in chapter 2, for many years lifetime employment in Japanese companies was a stable component of society. As one's initial employment essentially set one up for the rest of his (usually) or her life, being hired by the best possible company upon graduation from university became extremely important. Because of this pressure, most people in the past, and to a great extent today, believed that the key to a successful and stable future was a good education. A solid degree from a top-notch university would almost ensure recruitment and employment at a large, stable company. Therefore, the attainment of a degree from a well-known college or university became a goal of many families for their children.

But there was a trickle-down effect. In order to enter a good university, one had to graduate from a good high school and have high grades. Thus, the emphasis on graduating from a good university caused an increase in pressure to enter and succeed in a good high school. The trickle-down effect did not stop there, however. To enter a prestigious high school, one had to graduate with high marks from a good junior high, and so forth all the way down to preschool. Lifelong economic stability and contribution to society as a citizen pressured even young children to perform well.

This pressure did not stop at the school system. In order to help their children get ahead, many parents sent their children to preparatory schools, or juku, in the evenings or on weekends to help ensure their high performance on entrance exams and in regular school, so that they could graduate and move on and eventually win a place in a prestigious university. In this way, education, and more importantly academic performance, have come to consume the lives of many Japanese individuals from their very early, formative years through high school and university. It is not uncommon for these children and teenagers to study from morning to night, almost every day, in order to get ahead academically.

As an educator, I have nothing against a healthy emphasis on education and study in the family. Education is important for children and youth in order for them to become valued contributors to tomorrow's society. The educational system meets important socialization goals as well; school is where friendships are made and where young people learn how to deal with social problems and work out solutions.

Nevertheless, when education is emphasized as the sole element of one's existence, social consequences are inevitable. Children's whole lives revolve around study and grades. They spend the majority of their waking hours in school or juku and then at home studying. When children study to the almost total exclusion of all other kinds of learning experiences and social contact, they become "study robots," and problems in social development and morals are likely.

Kyoiku Mamas

Both parents are major contributors to this social epidemic. Many mothers—the so-called kyoiku mamas—raise their children with little emphasis on friendships and other normal and healthy relationships, even within the family. Success as mothers is intricately related to the success of the children in school and eventually in landing a good job. Ultimately, then, social success is equated with status and income. But the price for such achievement is high. Mothers, unaware of the dangers, pressure their children to excel academically, not realizing that their sons and daughters may also become social misfits.

Moreover, when behavioral problems occur, many kyoiku mamas are willing to ignore them as long as their child continues to study and earn good grades. Such exclusive emphasis on academic performance has led, essentially, to a blind spot in such mothers' view of the socialization of their children as social beings who need to learn to interact appropriately with others.

Many families opt to send their children to live away from home for the sake of education, thus exacerbating the problem. It is not uncommon, for example, for families to send their junior high and high school children to live in dorms run by schools. Although such living arrangements can provide valuable educational experiences, the children are denied the enormous benefits that the family itself can provide in the inculcation and development of a healthy self-concept, of social skills, and of morality.

For many years now I have been involved with educational and cultural exchange programs between the United States and Japan. While I do not have quantitative data, I have witnessed many instances where we have observed problems with Japanese students and their host families on these exchange programs. Many host families have reported to us that their Japanese students would not socialize with the family, would in fact lock themselves in their rooms rather than interact with the family, would forget even simple manners and fail to greet family members ("Good morning," "Good night," etc.), and would generally not fit in at home, oftentimes despite attempts by the host family to draw them out. When we have investigated these cases, we have often found that such problematic students have come from a dorm-living situation rather than from their family's home. Students who live in dorms for much of their young lives may, I believe, forget—or never learn—the basic social skills of living and interacting with family members (or at the very least, these skills may not have been reinforced). They may be excellent students academically, but there appears to be valuable experiential learning that is lost in the exclusive emphasis on academics.[10]

Many Japanese families send their children to live in dorms during junior high and high school not only for academic reasons but for other reasons as well, such as participation in sports clubs and teams. And although their abilities in those specific athletic activities may improve, there are social consequences to consider.

I also know of Japanese parents who send their elementary school-aged children abroad to receive an education that includes foreign language training. There are elite international schools in Japan as well. These families often have the economic resources and international connections that allow them to provide such "opportunities" for their children. Again, there may be benefit in language and academic skills training; however, one has to wonder whether such actions are beneficial to the development of the child as a whole person, especially at such a crucial stage in his or her psychological development.

Absentee Fathers

Fathers also contribute to this picture. Because fathers in the past two or three decades have spent most of their waking hours on the job, they have rarely spent time with their families.[11] The impact of this is major, because considerable research in developmental psychology has repeatedly demonstrated the importance of the father in the effective and appropriate socialization of his children in many social constructs, including social skills and morality.

When behavioral problems occur while their children are growing up, many fathers ignore them. Many of today's fathers are afraid to discipline their children, most likely because they feel guilty about not being at home very much to take care of them; because they feel sorry for their children, who are bottled up so much of the time studying; or because they want to have positive times and feelings with their children during what little time they have. Many such fathers engage in what I would call "popularity parenting."

Popularity parenting, however, often prohibits fathers (mostly) from providing moral and social guidance, discipline and punishment when needed, and boundary setting for their children. Hence, many contemporary Japanese fathers are not the moral beacons that they were the past. Developmental psychology has increasingly recognized the importance of such moral discipline and social training by both parents on the overall development of their children. In Japan, such responsibility has traditionally fallen on the shoulders of the fathers, and if they are not present or do not fulfill this role, their children often grow up with a lack of conscience about right and wrong, good and bad.

Thus, the societal pressures of education, which have reached epidemic proportions in many families over the years, the traditional views of marriage and work life, combined with other social factors, have produced a situation wherein many of Japan's youth today have grown up with little socialization training.

Many of these observations are supported by data. In the 1995 EPA study cited earlier, for example, the respondents were asked why they thought teaching children to behave properly has become more difficult over the years. The most common response was the emphasis on education. The next most common responses were that lifestyles have become more affluent and that parental authority has declined (Figure 3.4, page 120).

On top of this, one would think that attributing the cause of social problems to the emphasis on education would be strongest among those with less education, and that those individuals with higher educational degrees would probably not see the problems in education. In fact, however, the survey data indicate exactly the opposite; individuals with higher educational degrees actually see more problems in the emphasis on education than do people with lower educational achievements.

Most individuals surveyed believe that Japanese families are simply not doing their job in socializing the adults of tomorrow and in teaching the proper

Figure 3.4
Why Teaching Children to Behave Is More Difficult Today

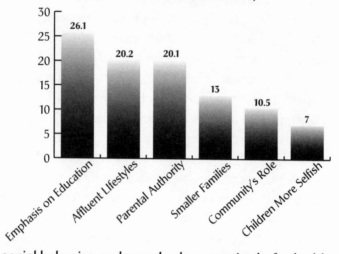

social behavior and moral values required of valuable citizens. When the data presented in Figure 3.3 on page 111 (which identifies the social values that most Japanese adults deemed lacking in Japanese youth) are examined and when the same respondents were asked whether these aspects of behavior should be instilled within the family environment, the evidence is irrefutable (Figure 3.5).

Given that most people surveyed believe that social values and skills should be instilled through the family and that the youth of Japan have problems in these specific areas, one can only reasonably conclude that most Japanese surveyed feel that families are simply not doing the all-important job of educating their children to become successful and valuable citizens.

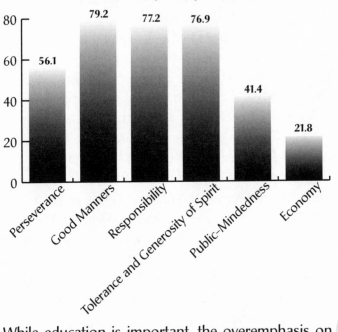

Figure 3.5
People Believing Social Skills
Are the Family's Responsibility

While education is important, the overemphasis on education and the academic pressures parents exert on their children from a very young age have undoubtedly contributed extensively not only to the cultural changes we have been discussing in this book, but also to the social and moral challenges that Japan faces today.

Social Factors

Social forces are also potential contributors to the changing moral values in contemporary Japanese society. For example, as the number of cars has increased and livable space has decreased, more families have decided not to allow their children to run and play outside with their friends because it is too dangerous. The possibility of kidnapping by strangers and other social crimes also contributes to this trend. Thus, children are becoming increasingly isolated from each other, losing valuable opportunities to learn about social appropriateness from others.

This tendency has had several negative consequences, in my view. First, when kids don't have the chance to run and roughhouse and use their bodies, they do not develop and mature as well physically as they could. When we are young, physical development is essential to mental, spiritual, and social development. Physical prowess is an important ingredient in self-confidence and discipline. With decreasing opportunities for play, children are not able to develop their bodies and their minds.

Play also contributes to the development of many important social skills. By developing friendships and even resolving fights with their peers, kids learn many valuable social skills. Unfortunately, in the current situation, where children are not allowed to develop these aspects of themselves because they cannot play outside as much as in the past, they do not learn the appropriate social and moral lessons that such interaction affords. Instead, they develop a strange sense of morality, in which even life and death have little more meaning than they would in a video game. Japan is not alone in this trend, of course. Witness the increase in juvenile violence in many Western developed nations in recent years, especially in the United States.

This leads to another point—the consequences of extensive use of video and computer games and the Internet. Despite all the positive outcomes associated with their development, they also contribute to this problem. Children today spend hour upon hour playing computer games, chatting with others via e-mail, or surfing the Internet. The rules that governed social etiquette, manners, and appropriateness are being thrown out the window in today's society as children carry on conversations with complete strangers, developing cyber relationships in lieu of real ones. The problems associated with excessive television viewing in the past are well documented; yet, interactive technology brings with it a new set of concerns.

The day prior to writing this passage, I heard on the news about two girls in Japan—one in high school, the other in junior high—who met on the Internet and became close in a cyber relationship. The high school girl was depressed about a relationship problem with a boy, so the younger girl jumped on a train to meet her in Kyushu (the junior high schooler lived in Nagoya), and together they jumped from a building out of despair. Events such as this point out the changes in moral values and the psychological numbing that occurs after long exposure to violent video games and other media.

Certainly, the mass media—television, comics, movies, and daily news—contribute to Japan's changing morality.[12] This includes the glamorization of the behaviors and lifestyles of professional athletes and entertainers, whose behavior the youth imitate. Their images, plus the products they display, are constantly projected to millions in ads on trains, on television, and in movies and magazines.

Thus, the major factors that are contributing to changing moral values in Japan include social as well as familial ones. Because they are so pervasive in Japanese society, their influence on changing culture and morality is beyond doubt. I do not believe the dominant cultural values and morality to be malicious in any way (although I realize that maliciousness certainly seems to be tolerated in many instances); instead, the current trend is to abandon previous stereotypic notions of culture and morality. Thus, contemporary Japanese moral values are not necessarily characterized by evil, but instead by an absence of good.

The Search for Morality among Japanese Youth

That many Japanese youth are not receiving training in social behavior or morality in their homes is a major concern for many. Morality gives all of us a sense of purpose and a philosophy of life. It gives us values that serve as guiding principles by which we can direct our thoughts, actions, opinions, and behaviors. It provides us with a sense of purpose and serves as a sort of bedrock or foundation, allowing for spiritual, emotional, and intellectual growth.

If many Japanese youth are not receiving training in social skills or morality, then exactly what kind of morality and value system do they have? In my observations, one value that many Japanese have adopted is materialism, the acquisition of money and expensive consumer goods. Quite frankly, the youth of Japan have come to treasure money and what it can buy. Again, I do not condemn the desire for such things; it is only natural in the commercial and capitalistic societies in which we—Japan, the United States, and most industrialized nations—live. What strikes me as peculiar is the meaning that this search for material goods has acquired in Japan.

One problem that is indicative of this social tendency among Japanese youth today is known as *enjo kosai*, or the young schoolgirls who go on dates and provide sex for money. In a 1998 survey by *Asahi Shimbun*, people were asked what they perceived to be the main contributing factors to this obvious social problem. The most common response was that "parents cannot discipline their children." The second most common response was that "society overemphasizes the desire for goods" (Figure 3.6, page 126).

Of course only a small proportion of young schoolgirls engage in this practice. But that such a practice exists at all is cause for concern over the heightened desire for money and goods. Thus, enjo kosai is

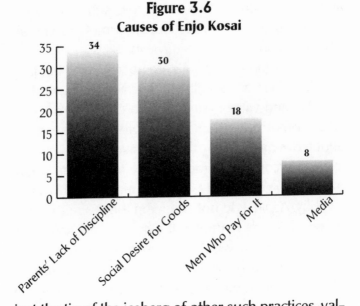

Figure 3.6
Causes of Enjo Kosai

just the tip of the iceberg of other such practices, values, and beliefs that are rooted in an emphasis on materialism.

Another indicator of the search for morality among contemporary Japanese youth is their desire for uniqueness. There is an overwhelming willingness to change—or at least tolerate changes in—some of the very characteristics that make the Japanese Japanese. For example, today it is not uncommon to walk around the streets of any major city in Japan and see young girls wearing platform shoes with soles so large and so high as to look ridiculous in relation to the rest of their bodies. It is also not uncommon to see both young boys and girls with their hair dyed all sorts of colors. Such statements indicate a desire to be unique or nonconformist and bear a remarkable resemblance to the youth fads in Western Europe and the United States.

Ijime (bullying) has increased alarmingly in the past decade or two and is apparently related to changes in cultural values and morality. Obviously, individuals who engage in bullying (or in so many of the other types of behaviors that are characteristic of the new Japan) are getting something out of this behavior. It fulfills some kind of psychological need that they have. The question I raise here is what need is being met? What are they searching for?

When we consider the complete picture I have painted of contemporary Japanese culture—greater functional psychological distances among people, greater resource availability, overemphasis on education, the lack of social etiquette and morality—I can only conclude that Japanese youth, lacking a sense of morality and conviction in their lives, are searching for spiritual fulfillment of some sort. Despite the glamor, glitz, money, and neon lights of major Japanese cities, there is an emptiness that is difficult to pinpoint. I think it has to do with a decline in spiritual meaning—in beliefs, philosophies, morality, grounding—that has occurred in association with the changing culture. This spiritual emptiness creates a longing that constantly begs for nourishment. Yet, the only nourishment it knows is through money, goods, and the constant search for uniqueness. Most people eventually find that such solutions are only temporary and cannot really address the deep-seated need for spiritual and moral nourishment that we all require. It is as if hungry people are being continually fed popcorn—lots of bulk but no nutritional value. And they remain essentially hungry, regardless of how much popcorn they eat.

The changes in Japanese culture that we have been exploring in the last two chapters have had drastic effects on society—business, interpersonal relationships, family life, educational systems and practices, and the like—and on culture, in the sense of our individual moralities and philosophies of life. The data presented so far are indisputable, as they represent the results from numerous research studies and surveys. Collectively, they speak loudly and clearly concerning the changes that have occurred in Japanese society and culture in recent history, and the consequences of those changes on the individuals who make up Japanese society. Growing cultural dualities and the diminishing moral base of society, left unchecked, do not bode well for the future. In chapter 4 we will explore some of the implications of such cultural changes.

Textnotes

[1] Here I refer to the American English usage of the term. I realize, however, that the connotations of the word in other languages may differ, even if they have a close semantic equivalent. Some languages, in fact, may not even have a word for culture as we know it.

2   I do recognize that "birthright" is often viewed by many Japanese as a necessary condition to being Japanese.

3   I do not mean to suggest that other similarities among the Japanese, including similarities in appearance and whatever biological or genetic overlaps may exist, are not important. They certainly contribute to an overall picture of the Japanese individual and culture, whether actual or perceived. I do believe, however, that the most important and salient aspects of being Japanese are those aspects that refer to functional, sociopsychological traits, including language, thoughts, behaviors, attitudes, values, shared histories, and the like. These aspects of culture are, to me, much more important and are the focus of my thesis here.

4   I do believe, however, that the sociopsychological construct of culture shares an intimate relationship with biology, affecting biology across time and generations, and vice versa.

5   Such conditions exist in many areas of the world today and throughout history, such as in rural areas of Central and South America, East and Southeast Asia, and certainly Japan in the past.

6   While individualism and collectivism may coexist, the type of individualism that may be witnessed in such societies is not the same as that practiced in predominantly individualistic societies because it is an individualistic pattern of behavior *superimposed* over an existing base of collectivism. Equating such a cultural pattern with individualism in traditional individualistic societies is, I believe, a mistake.

7   There is, of course, still an annual increase in the total population size. What I am saying here is that the degree to which population density changed is negligible when compared with the vast increase in resource availability due to increases in personal income.

8   It is also true that such technological advances in communication also bring people closer together. But I contend

that this is true only for the interactants of the communication. When a Japanese person speaks on his or her cellular phone in public amongst a crowd, it requires some degree of a lack of interpersonal consciousness among those people in the immediate area. Functional space is thereby created, which brings about decreases in population density functionally.

9 Another major factor contributing to Japan's cultural change not discussed here concerns the influence of the postwar educational system implemented by the American occupation forces. European- and American-based education is founded on a certain social and cultural rubric, and it fosters a way of thinking that is culturally appropriate for those countries but not for others (all educational systems are rooted in their home culture). This way of thinking is grounded in what may be termed "logical determinism," where theories are connected in a linear, cause-effect fashion. This way of thinking, as well as the other cultural products of the educational system imposed on Japan, probably made a large contribution to the cultural changes that have occurred in the country.

10 Certainly, many exchange students do well on their exchanges, forming new bonds and relationships with their host families.

11 This is related to the concept of *moretsu sarariman*, which describes the businessman who works feverishly for the company to meet demands and quotas, often from early morning to late at night.

12 Consider, for instance, the recent Japanese movie *Battle Royale*, in which teens are killed by a variety of gruesome and awful methods, and where "life is a game."

4

The Meaning of Changing Japanese Culture in Everyday Life

Changes in Japanese culture over the years have had many important implications regarding everyday life in Japan. We are all witness to the many difficulties, challenges, and obstacles that differences in thinking, attitudes, values, and behaviors bring to our work, play, and homes. Throughout this book, I have tried to build a case to suggest that many of these differences are occurring as a result of the growing cultural duality within the Japanese society—of growing individualism grafted onto a collectivistic base—and of changing moral values.

In this chapter, I examine four areas of our lives in which the changing Japanese culture is played out—work and business, sports, education, and everyday life. Cultural dualities are challenging existing social structures, social behavior, and rituals in all facets of life, forcing us to consider, and reconsider, the meaning of an evolving Japanese culture in people's lives.

The Japanese Business World

Clearly, corporate Japan has done an amazing job of rising from the economic ashes of World War II to enable Japan to become the major economic power that it has grown to be today. Japanese management practices, efficiency, manufacturing technology, and the psychology of the Japanese worker have been the marvel of the world for years and have been studied countless times by anthropologists, sociologists, psychologists, economists, politicians, and scientists in many other fields as well. Japanese products are known around the world as some of the best, if not the best, in their respective areas. Japanese conglomerates and affiliates are established in many countries, helping to contribute to local and national economies on many different levels.

Many of the changes in Japanese employees' attitudes, values, beliefs, and behaviors that we have discussed, however, illustrate that the Japanese business culture and organizational climate are profoundly different today from what they were in the past. These changes, in conjunction with the harsh economic realities in bottom-line profitability that many companies faced in the past decade, mean that Japanese companies and businesses must face many difficult challenges in the next several decades, not only to stay competitive and financially viable, but also to ensure maximum productivity among their workers and employees.

We have already seen some of the results of corporate Japan's answer to the cultural evolution occurring in Japan. Companies are instituting earlier retirement ages, offering fewer lifetime employment opportunities, and increasingly administering systems of wage and promotion based on merit, achievement, and ability rather than merely on seniority. These changes have not been easy to implement, because the previous systems of lifetime employment and salary based on seniority were rooted in a cultural rubric that was apropos for a previous Japanese society and which many people today still believe in.

The changing cultural values and the existence of cultural dualities in Japan bring with them a number of changes on the level of the individual worker as well. In this section, I briefly discuss several psychological consequences of the new cultural duality in Japan on the Japanese workforce.

The Meaning of and Attitudes toward Work and Companies

Some pillars of the Japanese character, as we have discussed throughout this book, were the notions of loyalty, commitment, sacrifice, and dedication to the ingroup. These values were some of the hallmarks of the stereotypic notions of Japanese culture that were inculcated from the time of the bushido warriors and that continued to be promoted in Japan after World War II. More recently, these values have been used to describe the Japanese worker in studies of industrial and organizational psychology, economics, and business management to explain the contributing factors of the rise of the Japanese economy.

The emerging cultural duality, however, is bringing about differences in these values, which, in turn, translate into real changes in behaviors. For example, people in different cultures hold different meanings of work. Workers in typically collectivistic cultures, such as the Japan of the past, tend to identify with their colleagues and with their company. In Japan the company and colleagues used to be fundamentally interrelated and became integral parts of the workers' self-identities. These tendencies were no doubt related to cultural differences in self-concept and manifested themselves in a variety of ways, such as the manner in which people identified themselves by company or organization first.[1] Bonds between colleagues and the company were strong and fundamentally and qualitatively different from those connectors for people with individual self-concepts from different cultures. In short, in the Japan of old, work, work colleagues, and the company became synonymous with the self.

People in individualistic cultures, however, have an easier time separating themselves from their jobs, and this tendency is working its way into the evolving Japanese culture. Workers find it easier to distinguish between "work time" and "personal time"; they make greater distinctions between company-based expense accounts and personal expenses; and they make greater distinctions between social and work activities with regard to both their work colleagues and their business associates (potential clients, customers, and so forth).

The changes in work values also mean that employees don't have to put their entire heart and soul into their current job and company, which is inevitable if they feel the company is not going to repay their efforts or offer lifetime employment. Workers are often not as willing to commit themselves to overtime work today, especially without compensatory pay. Overtime often cuts into personal enjoyment time or time with the family. In the past, workers were more willing to sacrifice their personal or family time for the sake of the company; now, however, the boundary between personal and company time is becoming clearer, and employees are more likely to protect their personal time. Overtime, which was one of the ways in which the Japanese worker bee demonstrated his or her commitment to and sacrifice for the company, was one of the major reasons why the Japanese economy succeeded to the degree that it did in the past.

Cultural differences in the meaning of work manifest themselves in other ways as well. In collectivistic cultures such as old Japan, work is seen as the fulfillment of an obligation to a larger group. Thus, in old Japan there was little movement of an individual from one company to another because of the individual's social obligations to the company to which he or she belonged and to colleagues.[2] In individualistic countries leaving one job (or even switching occupations) and going to another is easier because of the separation of the job from the self; a different job will accomplish the same goals. With the growing base of individualism in Japan today, mobility is also on the rise. With fewer prospects of lifetime employment in many companies, and with considerable dissatisfaction among workers about how their effort is being rewarded, more workers today are actively seeking opportunities in other companies while still employed by another. Such job searching while being employed was previously unheard-of in Japan.

Leadership and Management

Leadership and management styles have also been changing and are likely to continue to do so. For example, leaders and managers in the past were expected to look after their subordinates not only in terms of their work and life within the company, but of their private lives as well. Employees did not hesitate to consult with their bosses about problems at home and to seek advice from them. Leaders, more often than not, saw the need to help their subordinates with their private lives as an integral and important part of their jobs. It was not uncommon for Japanese bosses to find marriage partners for their subordinates and to look after them in personal ways, outside as well as inside the company.

Undoubtedly, one of the major reasons why this style of leadership existed is related to the meaning of work and the relationship between work and self in Japan in the past. As we discussed earlier, the boundaries between work and personal lives were not clear. Because the worker's existence at work became an integral part of the self, the distinction between work and company on the one hand and one's personal life on the other was blurred. Essentially, work *was* one's life. Thus, leaders took care of their employees much as parents would take care of their children. There was a bond between them that extended well beyond the company.

In contemporary Japan, however, such expectations and behaviors are changing, in large part because of the changing Japanese culture. As workers begin to draw sharper distinctions between their personal lives and work, the boundaries between self and family on the one hand and work, company, and colleagues on the other become greater. Efforts by superiors to intervene in the lives of their subordinates are more often than before being looked upon as interference or an intrusion on privacy. The only "legitimate" area of intervention by a superior in the life of a subordinate is slowly becoming that which is defined by the job itself, and the legitimate time of such intervention is slowly being accepted as work hours only.[3] As Japanese culture continues to change, management and leadership style will surely continue to evolve as well.

One Japanese psychologist, Jyuji Misumi, has provided a framework by which we can understand such changes in leadership, management, and supervision associated with culture (Misumi and Peterson [1985]). He suggests that management involves general and universal functions that all effective leaders must carry out, but that the manner in which they are dispatched can vary. He then contrasts functions related to task performance and group maintenance and suggests that both domains involve universal leadership goals that are consistent across cultures and companies. Different specific behaviors may be used to accomplish these managerial goals, however, depending on situations, companies, and cultures.

While both functions are relevant to all leaders, Japanese companies in the past were characterized by a greater emphasis on group maintenance than on task performance. Of course, performance has always been important in companies, but the collectivistic nature of Japanese culture in the past also meant that task performance must be balanced by a great degree of group maintenance activities. This emphasis is related, in my mind, to Japan's previous emphasis on harmony.

The changing Japanese culture, however, means that such an emphasis on harmony may not be as strong today as it was in the past.[4] Thus, leadership behaviors may be more focused on task performance than on group maintenance. This means that the nature of leadership and supervision is changing from

one of a family-oriented leader to one of content spe-
cialization and task specificity.

Many of these differences between previous and
contemporary conceptualizations of leadership are
reflected in a newspaper article about Makoto Naruke,
former president of Microsoft Japan (*Japan Times*, 11
March 2001). The article described Naruke as a "perverse" individualist who embraces opportunity where
others see gloom, and "who avoids following the
crowd and does things that others dare not." In fact
when the firm's sales increased nineteenfold during
his tenure, his interest in the job faded:

> Microsoft was fun in the beginning because the
> firm was very unique back then.... But now there
> are many others doing the same. It's not that I
> want to become No. 1 among many. I would
> rather be one of a very few, if not the one and
> only.... When you keep doing one thing for
> some time, don't you get tired? If you do, you
> can just quit. It's so easy now.... Even if you
> don't know what you want to do next, you can
> live on part-time jobs till you find out what you
> really want to do. (1)

This clearly doesn't sound like the voice of a typical
Japanese leader of the past. It reflects the change in
Japanese culture that is permeating corporate Japan
today.[5]

Motivation and Productivity

One of the most interesting findings in social
psycholoogy research in the United States is that group

productivity often declines in larger groups (Latane, Williams, and Harkins 1979). These findings have contributed to the coining of the expression "social loafing." Two factors appear to contribute to this phenomenon, at least in the U.S. One is the reduced efficiency resulting from the loss of coordination among workers' efforts; as group membership increases, presumably the lack of coordination among people reduces efficiency, resulting in the lack of activity or duplicate activity, which in turn results in the loss of productivity. The second factor involves the reduction in effort by individuals when they work in groups as compared with when they work by themselves. B. Latane and his colleagues (Latane, Williams, and Harkins 1979) have conducted a number of studies investigating group size, coordination, and effort and have found that in larger groups, a lack of both coordination and effort resulted in decreased productivity. Latane (1981) attributed these findings to a diffusion of responsibility in groups. That is, as group size increases, the responsibility for getting a job done is divided among more people, and many group members ease up because their individual contribution is less recognizable.

Previous cross-cultural research in Japan, however, indicated that exactly the opposite phenomenon occurred there. For instance, Sanshiro Shirakashi (1985) and Susumu Yamaguchi, Koichi Okamoto, and Takashi Oka (1985) conducted studies involving Japanese participants performing several tasks. They showed that not only did social loafing not occur but that being in a group actually enhanced individual performance for their subjects. P. Christopher Earley (1989) and William Gabrenya, Y. Wang, and Latane (1985) noted a similar phenomenon in samples of Chinese school-children. This opposite effect has been called "social striving" and has been claimed by many writers as one factor that has contributed to the postwar economic success of Japan.

Writers typically speculated that social striving occurs in cultures like Japan and China because of their collectivistic nature. Because collectivism fosters inter-personal interdependence and group collective functioning more than individualistic cultures do, groups tend to be more productive in these cultures precisely because they foster coordination among ingroup members. They also place higher values on individual contributions in ingroup settings.

Changes in Japanese culture, however, suggest that social striving and its positive contribution to productivity may not ring as true now or in the future. As traditional collectivism diminishes and is replaced by individualistic tendencies, especially among much of the younger workforce, one may expect a resulting decrease in social striving and an increase in social loafing. If so, these changes mean that leadership and supervisory styles need to change in order to deal with changes in productivity that are caused by changing Japanese culture.

These notions are bolstered by the studies conducted by Toshio Yamagishi described in chapter 2.

You will remember that Yamagishi conducted two studies in which American and Japanese students participated in small groups that required cooperative behavior to perform a task (Yamagishi 1988a, b). When a system of mutual monitoring and social sanctions existed for individual participation in the group, the Japanese students did indeed contribute more to the group than did the Americans. But when the system of monitoring and sanctions was eliminated, it was the Americans, not the Japanese, who contributed more. In fact, more Japanese chose to leave the group than did Americans. American participants had higher levels of trust and cooperation in this condition, and there were no differences between Americans and Japanese in their contributions to the provision of a sanctioning system. Clearly, these types of findings raise questions about whether or not previous traditional, stereotypic views of the Japanese worker-bee productivity will be valid now or in the future.

Other Areas of Work

Many other aspects of work, beyond those discussed so far, are changing as well. Take, for instance, interpersonal relations. Workers nowadays are more distant toward their work colleagues because of the reduced emphasis on harmony, and greater distinctions are drawn between oneself and one's peers in the company. Increasing individualism also brings with it less status differentiation. Thus, employees do not have the blind trust in and loyalty to their bosses and superiors that they had in the past, and they are less afraid to question authority.

Increasing individualism also brings with it an increased recognition of individual differences and less distinction between the sexes. This is a particularly interesting trend. When Geert Hofstede did his well-known studies of cultural differences in work-related values (Hofstede 1980, 1984), the Japanese were ranked the highest on the cultural dimension of Masculinity, which also meant the greatest distinctions between the sexes. Individualism, however, promotes an awareness of the merit and uniqueness of each individual, regardless of gender (at least theoretically). Thus, awareness about sexual discrimination and harassment is on the rise in Japan, along with the growing awareness that men and women should be treated as equals, which is a direct consequence of individualism. In the 1999 EPA survey conducted by the Japanese government, the majority of men and women of all ages who were surveyed felt that sex discrimination exists in Japan (see Figure 4.1 in the Appendix).

Although the trend is slow, more women are rising to positions of leadership in all areas of Japanese companies and government. And along with this trend, demeaning tasks and responsibilities, such as that of the typical tea lady of the past, are slowly being eradicated.

Finally, increased individualism is also resulting in an increased ability to think creatively and critically. Thus, individuals in Japanese companies are able to think creatively about ways to deal with the problems that companies face due to recession and other economic crises. This is due in part to the emphasis within individualism on creativity, autonomy, and uniqueness. When Japan was a more homogeneous, collectivistic culture, such creativity was rarer, was not sought out, and was not rewarded.[6]

Summary

These, and many other changes in the individual psychologies and behaviors of Japanese employees, are natural and inevitable consequences of the changes in Japanese culture that we have discussed. In Table 4.1, I summarize these and other possible changes in work-related values, attitudes, and behaviors, contrasting stereotypic attitudes of the past with those of the present and the future. As tensions continue to rise between traditional and contemporary views of work, worker relations, and personnel and labor management systems, they continue to challenge an already strained corporate and labor system that is struggling for survival against worldwide competition. Thus, corporate Japan faces not only external competition, but internal struggles as well. Inevitably, Japan will not be able to face its external competition well if it does not adequately and satisfactorily address the needs and challenges brought about by its internal factors.

Table 4.1
Some Possible Alterations in Work-Related Values, Attitudes, and Behaviors in a Culturally Changing Japan*

Japan in the Past	Japan Now and in the Future
Reliance on the company to provide for the employee	Lower expectation the company will provide for the employee
Sacrificing personal time for the company	Importance of employees' personal time
Large companies attractive	Small companies attractive
Moral involvement with the company	Self-serving involvement with the company
Moral importance attached to training and use of skills in jobs	More importance attached to freedom and challenge in jobs
Managers aspire to conformity and orderliness	Managers aspire to leadership and variety
Managers rate having security in their position as important	Managers rate having autonomy as important
Managers support "traditional" points of view, not employee initiative and group activity	Managers endorse "modern" points of view, employee initiative and group activity
Group decisions better than individual ones	Individual decisions better than group ones
Managers choose duty, expertise, and prestige as goals	Managers choose pleasure, affection, and security as goals
Individual initiative is socially frowned upon	Individual initiative is socially encouraged
Social relationships predetermined by ingroups	Need to make specific friendships
Managers make decisions auto–cratically and paternalistically	Managers make decisions after consulting with subordinates
Employees fearful of disagreeing with their boss	Employees less afraid of disagreeing with their boss
Companies' interference in private life accepted	Companies' interference in private life rejected
Higher job stress	Lower job stress
Fewer women in jobs; less mixed sex composition	More women in jobs; more mixed sex composition

* Adapted from Geert Hofstede's *Culture's Consequences: International Differences in Work-Related Values*, 166–67.

The Educational System

Since the end of World War II, Japan's educational system has been one of the strongest pillars of society. There is no doubt about the quality of the education of the average Japanese student. Many international studies in educational psychology that have compared academic and scholastic skills and aptitudes of students around the world consistently rank Japanese students at the top or near the top in almost every field measured. This is especially true in subjects such as math and science.[7]

The substantial difference in the quality of education between the United States and Japan is reinforced for me every year when my family hosts high school students from Japan on homestay cultural exchange programs. These students come to the U.S. for two or three weeks and are required to attend high school with their host families' high school students. Inevitably, they tell me that much of American school life is boring, especially math.[8] When I ask them why, they always tell me the same thing—the math American high school students are struggling with is math the Japanese students learned in junior high, and in some cases, in elementary school.

The same is true for English grammar. At San Francisco State University, where I teach full-time, students from many different countries, including Japan, take my courses. Many students (but not all) write English with a surprising degree of proficiency, which often impresses me. When my daughter receives letters in English from her Japanese friends, I often think that their written English is better than many native English speakers' English. Of course, not every Japanese university or high school student has great English skills. But I cannot even imagine the typical American high school or university student coming close to writing a letter or a paper in another language.

The evolving Japanese culture that we have been discussing has broad and far-reaching implications for the Japanese educational system. In the following sections I discuss some of the issues and problems that Japanese education faces; I believe most are directly related to the changing Japanese culture and emerging cultural dualities.

Student Attitudes

One major problem that Japanese institutions of higher education face, for instance, concerns the behaviors and attitudes of many of their university students. My colleagues tell me many stories about Japanese students who come to class only to sleep, talk with their friends, or daydream. In many instances, students will leave their cellular phones on during class, answer them if they ring, and actually have telephone conversations with others during lecture!

Certainly, not all university students act like this. I have taught in Japanese universities and have been pleasantly surprised at the high level of motivation and interest shown by the students to learn the material presented.[9] Nonetheless, it is true that students do exhibit the behaviors described above, and I cannot help but think that such behavior is entirely contradictory to how Japanese students of the past would have been even if they had had such gadgets as cellular phones.

There have also been major changes in students' attitudes toward achievement and academic success. Students today are much more likely to attribute their achievements and success to their own aptitudes and abilities. In the past students would have been more likely to acknowledge the contributions of those around them, such as their teachers, family members, and the like. Students today are less likely to acknowledge such external contributions to their achievements. When teachers and family members, however, expect such acknowledgment and do not receive it, the result can be strife and conflict.

Increasing individualism in Japanese culture has, in part, brought about such changes in students' attitudes. Attribution concerning achievement and success, for instance, is a well-studied area in social psychology, and it has been well documented in the past that attributing success to internal factors (e.g., one's effort, ability, degree of study, etc.) is the norm in individualistic cultures. In collectivistic cultures, however, students are more likely to attribute academic success to external factors (e.g., the kindness of the people around them, luck, fate, etc.). Because Japan has moved from a socially homogeneous, collectivist culture to that of a duality that includes individualism, it is no wonder that such attributional styles are emerging.

This emerging cultural duality also contributes to changing student attitudes in classrooms and in everyday interactions with teachers, as described above. As we discussed in chapter 3, the evolving Japanese culture is also associated with changes in morality; even basic rules of politeness and social etiquette are quickly being overturned. There is less of a sense of interpersonal consciousness and harmony. Thus behaviors that threaten to disrupt group functioning, such as what occurs in many classrooms today, have emerged.

Of course, economic realities also enter into this picture. Population statistics reveal that the number of young people entering colleges and universities will decrease dramatically over the next ten years. If universities and colleges are too strict in grading their students, resulting in a higher failure rate, potential new recruits will seek admission to other, less rigorous schools. If this occurs, universities with high academic standards will be faced with declining enrollments and financial difficulties. Thus, there is pressure among the faculty and administration to ease up on academic standards to allow students to pass and graduate, despite the obviously failing quality of academic work. This, coupled with the perceived ease of graduation from Japanese universities, is also a challenge for the Japanese educational system and society in the future.

Bullying

One of the worst problems facing the Japanese educational system—and the families that must be involved with it—is ijime. While it is nothing new, ijime appears to be on the rise over the past decade or so. I cannot help but think that problems such as this are increasing at least in part because of the overemphasis on education; the pressures that teachers, parents, and society put on students regarding study and grades; and the lack of moral and social behavior training in families today. Japanese culture is unique not so much in the fact that it is changing but because these changes have occurred with incredible speed and with a drastic change in moral values among many of the Japanese youth.

Data compiled by the Japanese government[10] shows unequivocally the steady increase in bullying in the schools today. See the data on juvenile arrests for matters related to bullying from 1991 to 1995 (Figure 4.2).[11] These data do not reflect everyday bullying problems that do not lead to arrests, such as the oftentimes verbal, and sometimes physical, abuse of students by students.

In some instances, cases of physical abuse directly related to bullying have led to severe consequences. In some clubs, for example, I know of several instances of abuse by *sempai* (senior member) to *kohai* (junior member) that have led to death. Such extreme degrees of abuse seem to be more frequent nowadays, and I

Figure 4.2
**Number of Juvenile Arrests for
Bullying and Related Matters**[12]

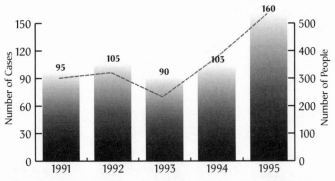

interpret such disturbing trends as due to a deterioration of moral values among youth today in Japan.

Dropouts

Another major problem in relation to the educational
system concerns the widespread occurrence of dropouts. Currently, many students are dropping out of
school, and this trend has been on the rise over the
past decade. As can be seen in the data compiled by
the Japanese government and represented in Table 4.2,
this trend is evident in junior high and elementary
school.

Many observers comment that there are multiple
reasons for this large increase in dropouts, including
anxiety, emotional disturbance, juvenile delinquency,
a desire to have fun, or apathy. I interpret these data
as being directly related to the changing Japanese
culture and the emergence of cultural dualities. In ad-

Table 4.2
Dropout Rates for Elementary,
Junior High, and High Schools

Year	Elementary School	Junior High	High School
1991	12,645	54,172	112,933
1992	13,710	58,421	101,194
1993	14,769	60,039	94,065
1994	15,786	61,663	96,401
1995	16,569	65,022	98,179
1996	19,498	74,853	111,989
1997	20,765	84,701	111,491
1998	26,017	101,675	111,372
1999	26,047	104,180	Not available

dition many observers suggest that students nowadays cannot adjust well to school life, which leads to
problems such as dropping out of school or ijime. In
other words, families are not adequately preparing
their children for adjustment to life outside the home
environment. When they enter school, these children
encounter a system that is based on the previous, collectivistic Japanese culture. That is, the educational
system itself—including its administrative structure;
teaching methodologies; teacher attitudes, values, and
beliefs; student-teacher ratios; the physical layout of
classrooms; and so on—are all manifestations and
products of a certain cultural period, corresponding
to previous, stereotypic notions of Japanese culture
and society that are not congruent with society today.
As such, when students enter school, they are con-
fronted with a major cultural clash. Because many
children and youth do not yet have the emotional or

psychological skills to weather such conflict and do not receive guidance in how to resolve them, they either drop out or find other ways to cope with their stress, including bullying and juvenile delinquency.

Juvenile Delinquency

The changing Japanese culture has also brought about increases in juvenile delinquency, which in turn is associated with minor and major crimes and the use of drugs. While not directly related to education per se, I include this discussion here because I believe that these data reflect, in part, problems within the educational system brought about by cultural dualities.

As can be seen in Figure 4.3, juvenile arrests for criminal delinquency span a range of activities, the most common of which involve some kind of larceny or theft.

Figure 4.3
Juvenile Arrests[13]

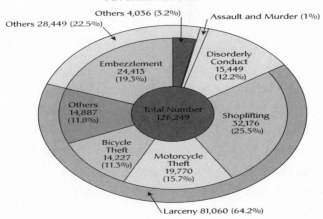

Others 4,036 (3.2%)   Assault and Murder (1%)

Others 28,449 (22.5%)

Embezzlement 24,413 (19.3%)

Disorderly Conduct 15,449 (12.2%)

Others 14,887 (11.8%)

Total Number 126,249

Shoplifting 32,176 (25.5%)

Bicycle Theft 14,227 (11.3%)

Motorcycle Theft 19,770 (15.7%)

Larceny 81,060 (64.2%)

When broken down by age, an interesting picture emerges (Figure 4.4). The ages during which the greatest number of criminal delinquency activities are occurring is between 15 and 16 years of age. This corresponds to the age range at which students move from junior high to high school in Japan.

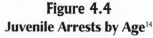

Figure 4.4
Juvenile Arrests by Age[14]

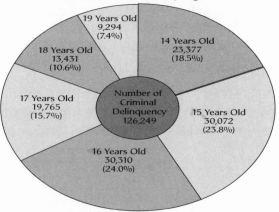

As we have discussed, I believe these data reflect, in part, student attempts to cope with the stress brought about by emerging cultural dualities. The cultural clashes between the old (some may say archaic) educational system and contemporary societal and cultural values, and the resulting lack of moral guidance among the youth, stress the system and bring about some of the consequences we are witness to today.

Family Attitudes

A friend of mine told me once about her experiences with a Japanese parent–teacher association (PTA) at a school in Japan. The PTA members were upset because their children/students were exhibiting and experiencing more and more problems in school, including some of the problems we have discussed here. Yet their basic approach was, essentially, to look to the schools to provide moral education for their students.

While I do agree that education should be dispensed in a manner that brings about morally appropriate behaviors as outcomes, I am not at all sure that schools should be the primary moral socialization agents for children or that parents should look to schools to do that for them. It is akin to what is happening in many areas of the United States, where parents look to schools to protect their children from violence or to instill the value of studying and obtaining an education in the first place. In my experience, it is very difficult for schools, or any other system outside of the family, to have such an impact on their members if the families do not hold the same values and goals and become the primary enculturation agents. For families, whether Japanese or American, to look to schools to instill such basic values in their students is a misplaced attribution of responsibility.

This attributional style on the part of parents and families is due, in part, to the changing cultural rubric of Japan. The attribution of responsibility described here is a tendency that is exhibited in other individualistic cultures; thus many of today's parents exhibit such tendencies, as do their children. In addition, many parents still appreciate the value of an education only to the extent that their children do well on tests, as we discussed in chapter 3, and depreciate the moral and character development of their children in the process.

Individualized Attention and Its Implications for Educational Reform

There are other consequences of social and cultural changes that are not as dramatic as ijime and juvenile delinquency. For example, increasing individuality among students and families has brought about an increasing awareness and perceived need for individualized attention and instruction. Accordingly, one of the goals of the Japanese government's educational reform plan[15] is to lower the student–teacher ratio to 20:1. Such a trend is entirely counter to the prevailing Japanese educational practice of large student–faculty ratios and group–oriented teaching methods that are well documented in international studies of education and educational psychology. If such trends continue, they will in time force educational practices, pedagogy, methodology, and even curriculum to change.

The current and previous Japanese educational systems have been excellent at producing students who can excel in academic material requiring rote memorization. Yet it has not done well at fostering other thinking skills, such as creativity or critical thinking. Many Japanese youth today, with their essentially individualistic natures, have a need to be creative and to think critically. Thus they are frustrated with the Japanese system that discourages these skills in favor of rote memorization of facts. This is yet another example of the cultural clash that the youth of Japan are experiencing today and that will undoubtedly lead to curriculum reform. Such changes in curricula, moreover, will in turn lead to changes in teacher training, methodologies, and basic aspects of the Japanese educational system in the future.

Summary

There are many other differences in student and family behaviors associated with the changing Japanese culture. The interaction between these evolving cultural characteristics and the overemphasis on education, on the one hand, and the underemphasis on moral and social development on the other, promise to provide obstacles to the Japanese educational system for years to come. To a large extent, these issues are similar to those being faced in many countries and societies of the world. The real issue concerns the degree to which the Japanese can treat these obstacles as challenges, thus turning them to their favor.

Sports

In any culture sports serves as a stage from which cultural values, and important changes in cultural values, can easily be witnessed. Sports in all of its facets is value laden, and we can observe those values in athlete training and competition, team and individual activities on and off the field of play, and in society's reactions and attitudes toward sports and athletes. Star athletes play a central role in illuminating social values; they set the stage for appropriate and inappropriate behavior, values, attitudes, beliefs, and opinions, all of which are communicated via mass media to the rest of society. Because youth attempt to emulate star athletes, the athletic world plays a major part in molding culture as well as modeling it. For these reasons, and as an example of more generalized social change, I examine here how Japanese cultural changes have occurred as witnessed through sports.

Competition and the Olympic Ideals

Competition is at the heart of any sport, whether it be team or individual, against others, or against a clock. In English the etymology of the word *competition* actually stems from a Latin word meaning "to seek" and "to rise together." That is, the original meaning of *competition* suggests that competitors come to the playing field not only to see who is better but also to rise together, to complement each other in improving themselves. Self-improvement through competition should occur not only in athletic skills but also, or more importantly, in interpersonal skills. In other words, competition is supposed to bring out the best in all of us as people; it should teach us respect for each other, humility in our own limitations, cooperation with team-mates, and hard work—many of the values that we can strive for in the other aspects of our lives.

It was with this intent that Baron Pierre de Coubertin of France restarted the modern Olympic Games. His goal was to use the Olympics as a method for bringing countries together, for however short a period of time, and to use sports to put differences aside, to learn about each other, and to improve the world. In this way, the modern Olympic movement was founded with the pinnacle of sporting ideals in mind.

Nowadays I cannot help but think sometimes that we have wandered far from this meaning of competition. This is true, of course, in the United States, the acknowledged home of professional sports in the world. Unfortunately, sports in the U.S. has quickly eroded from a complementary system of moral education through physical activity to a world governed by cash and by win-lose thinking. Nowhere is this more clearly evident than in professional sports. This saddens me, because it seems that those athletes who are truly at the top of their respective sports and thus serve as role models for all youth should be the ones to model the values, attitudes, and behaviors represented in the original meaning of competition: consideration for others, respect, humility, discipline, and self-restraint. The highest-level athletes should be the best representatives of the virtue of a country or culture. They should be the model citizens of their society. They should, through rising and coming together through competition, be universal symbols of a better world.

Instead, the professional sports arena seems to be characterized by selfishness, greed, rudeness, and arrogance, especially in the United States. Witness the violent behavior that some basketball players exhibit to their coaches, and yet they are allowed to continue to play basketball at a considerable salary. Witness boxers who bite their opponents, who are convicted of heinous crimes, and who nevertheless remain stars in the public's eye. Witness baseball players who can make comments in the press that many interpret as racial slurs and yet be treated as heroes by many others. And those professional athletes who do espouse the moral virtues as originally expounded in the Olympic movement are portrayed by the press as anomalies, not typical role models.

Celebrity sports has real-life social consequences. For instance, many of our youth are learning that they don't have to study in school, that getting a good education is not important, but being good at sports is. Sports has become an end in itself rather than a means to a higher end. Students learn that winning is everything, and that as long as they win, they can do anything they want, say anything they want, and be anything they want. The youth are learning that they don't have to be in school in the first place, or that it is merely a temporary place to develop their athletic skills until they can make it into the professional ranks later on. If they can hone their basketball or football or base-ball skills, they may have a chance to play in the pros and be set financially for life.

But alas, for every one person who makes it to the professional level, there are thousands and thousands who do not. In this reverse way, the glorification of sports and athletes may be part of the problem, not part of the solution.

Sports and the Japanese

My experiences with Japanese athletes and sport groups in the past led me to believe that the Japanese competitor was a person of high moral standards, a symbol of what was best about the people of his or her country. I believed this person had strong moral convictions, engaged in fair play, and believed his or her opponent to be worthy of the highest respect. Competition was marked by valor and dignity. Rules of engagement encouraged these unspoken laws of morality, and athletes followed a certain protocol, win or lose. While there was certainly individual and group pride, there was also respect for others and for the competition itself. Winning was certainly important, and I do not suggest that it shouldn't be important today as well, but winning and losing were not the only things that mattered. When athletes won, they showed restraint and respect for the feelings of their opponents. When they lost, they showed humility and acceptance. There was valor not only in victory, but also in defeat.[16] The Japanese were great warriors, not only in the sense of competition and results, but also in terms of the way they carried themselves as citizens of their country and of the world. Like many people, I respected these great warriors as well as their philosophy and way of life.

As Japanese culture changes, however, so does Japanese sports. Watching Japanese athletes nowadays, I don't feel the respect for them that I did in the past. Sure, some athletes model the athlete of the past. But for every time I see a Japanese athlete who carries him- or herself with great dignity, I see many others who do not. This is true in professional sports and in amateur sports in Japan.

Judo

The sport I know best, judo, is itself rife with such social change.[17] Even though judo is a vestige of moral training derived from *budo* (systems of moral and intellectual education), these virtues and values of the past do not seem to be carried on in training and competition. Japanese judo, at least the way it seems to me, has bought into the commercialism of international sports, and in large part judo athletes perceive their sport solely in terms of winning and losing (i.e., not as an art with the main goal of developing character). Traditional judo, which included moral and intellectual education, has lost its meaning because the Japanese have come to see winning in competition as the only viable option that determines or defines their self-worth and that of the Japanese people. Winning is more important than being a role model for the youth of Japan or honoring the image and valor of the country through sport.

For example, I often witness international judo matches and practices around the world. At the highest level of competition, it is very difficult to tell the difference between the skill levels of athletes. If you go to any average judo dojo anywhere in the world, however, and compare it with any average judo dojo in Japan, you would be shocked to see that non-Japanese who practice judo display the behaviors, values, and practices of moral discipline and manners that are associated with traditional judo, but the Japanese often do not. Many Japanese judo instructors who visit other countries to teach judo similarly observe that although skill and ability levels are generally higher in Japan, the values, ethics, and moral teachings associated with judo are often better preserved in other countries. In fact, this is one of the reasons why judo is so popular in other countries—because it is not seen solely as a sport.

One possible reason for this trend may be that judo teachers are not instilling traditional values in their students. Or, I wonder, perhaps this trend is simply a product of those among the youth generation in Japan who are actually competing. Recently, my colleagues and I completed an interesting study on the values of judo coaches and teachers in the United States, Poland, and Japan (Matsumoto, Takeuchi, and Horiyama 2001). These coaches and instructors completed three lengthy values surveys. One of them measured six different scales: individuality, achievement, patriotism, honor, justice, and spiritual balance. When we examined the differences among the countries on these six scales, we were surprised to find that Americans and Poles had significantly higher scores than the Japanese on patriotism, honor, justice, and spiritual balance. The Japanese, however, had higher scores on achievement and individuality (Figure 4.5).

Figure 4.5
Values Differences among Judo Coaches

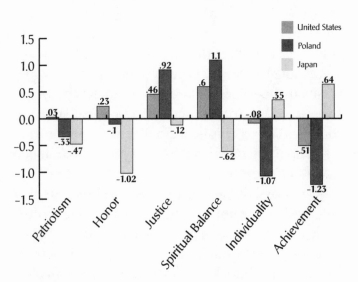

These data are simply amazing to me, and they indicate that, even in a sport that has its roots in Japanese budo, the primary emphasis of judo coaches in Japan is on individuality and achievement. It seems to me that judo in the other countries has retained much more of its original meaning than it has in Japan.[18]

In another study conducted by my colleagues and me (Takeuchi, Wakayama, Okada, and Matsumoto, 2001), we administered the Intercultural Adjustment Potential Scale (ICAPS) to 570 Japanese university students of judo in Japan. The ICAPS is a scale that measures the ability of an individual to adjust to life in a different culture. In doing so, it measures four basic psychological skills that are considered necessary for successful adjustment—emotion regulation, openness, flexibility, and autonomy. The reason we chose this test to administer to Japanese students of judo is that these psychological skills are precisely those that are supposedly improved in the character development aspects of the art of judo. Despite these assumptions, however, the data indicated that those involved in judo had significantly lower overall scores than those who were not, and drastically lower scores on emotion regulation. This latter finding is especially crucial to this discussion, because emotion regulation is a key component of self-discipline, one of the outcomes that is supposed to develop through the practice of judo.[19]

My observations of an event that happened at and after the 2000 Olympic Games in Sydney are also an eye-opener. Many sporting fans around the world know of the famous judo match between two national favorites—David Douillet of France and Shinichi Shinohara of Japan.[20] During this match, there was a controversial action that looked as if either opponent could score. In fact, if called in Douillet's favor, the score would have been minor; if it had been Shinohara's score, however, it would have been an *ippon*, which is the equivalent of a knockout in boxing, and would have ended the match. The outcome of the three referees' judgments was a score for Douillet. The match thus continued. Douillet actually gained other points during the remainder of the match, but Shinohara did not, and Douillet eventually won the match and the gold medal.

This match resulted in an uproar from the Japanese judo contingent and the Japanese public. The Japanese coaching staff protested the outcome of the call and the match, and the Japanese media went berserk in portraying the "unfairness" of the match and the "problem" with the referees.[21]

What happened after this match was over, however, is the point of this story. That evening the e-mail boxes of the International Judo Federation and of many of its members and officers were flooded by messages, mainly from Japan, protesting this call. While that in itself is not surprising, what was surprising was the tenor and manner in which these messages were delivered. Quite frankly, there were hundreds of vicious, personal attacks against the organization and specific individuals. The slanderous and outrageous personal attacks were carried on for months. By far, the bulk of this mail came from Japan.

The referee who officiated the controversial match received the brunt of these attacks. In addition to personal attacks on his character, he also received many death threats, and in one case actually received a doll that was cut in half and mailed to his house. The doll was mailed from Japan. He eventually had to vacate his home for several weeks because the Japanese press had found out where he lived and had camped outside his house.

Who won or lost is really not the point in this story. What saddens me is the way so many Japanese decided to carry on a personal vendetta against others because of the loss and because of the manner in which judo leaders in Japan permitted it to happen. The manner in which this entire episode unfolded was, to me, evidence of the lack of moral virtue and values that characterized Japan in the past. Being saddened at the outcome, outraged at the perceived unfairness of a referee call, or frustrated with the loss are all acceptable and understandable. Death threats, however, cross the line between acceptable and not. It is, as we have been discussing throughout this book, evidence of the changing nature of Japanese culture.

Summary

I am sure that these trends witnessed in judo are not limited to that sport alone but are true in many others in Japan; they reflect the great social and cultural evolution of the time, and are not endemic to any single sport. As sports has become very commercialized, it is difficult not to think of sports solely in terms of winning and losing. On television, for example, we are constantly witness to many sports champions before and after competition. But how often are athletes asked to appear on television because of their moral values and their overall worth as people and role models, even if they have lost their matches? Not very often. As I discussed above, these trends have major implications for society and for the training and preparation of our youth for the future. Of course, not all judo instructors are like those I've described above, and not all coaches, instructors, mentors, and athletes in many other sports are like them, either.[22] Yet, these trends do describe a large segment of Japan's dynamically changing population.

Changing Japanese Culture and Everyday Life

As I have discussed throughout this book, traditional Japanese culture has been the marvel of social scientists for decades. Values such as perseverance, respect, loyalty, politeness, frugality, modesty, and the like were the hallmarks of a society that was, and in many ways still is, considered the jewel of civilization. Interpersonal relationships were warm, friendly, and cordial; the family was the strongest unit of society, and the relationship between parent and child was the model held for many other relationships.

Yet values such as perseverance are eroding in daily life. People are becoming increasingly impulsive, quicker to lose control of their emotions. The inability to control one's feelings and impulses has had major consequences for society, as in the problem with ijime in the schools. The data presented above concerning ICAPS scores of Japanese students of judo also speaks to the inability to control one's emotions among this group of individuals.

Frugality is being replaced by excessiveness. Extravagance, luxury, and convenience are landmarks of this new lifestyle. In particular, the values of materialism and commercialism, as well as the increasing need for uniqueness that is associated with individualism, are major contributors to the current trend toward extravagance. In fact, many studies in social and cross-cultural psychology have demonstrated an empirical relationship between the value of individualism on the country level and materialism and commercialism. Why? Capitalist countries with free-market economies, such as Japan and the United States, tend to foster all three of these values. When considered in this manner, the opening of Japan with the Meiji Restoration along with the effects of the occupation after World War II (especially education reform) have had important cultural consequences to Japan that perhaps could not have been foreseen at those times.

One of the hallmarks of traditional Japan was politeness. In fact, much of Japanese culture and society could be understood in terms of institutionalized politeness, as reflected in its many rituals. New Year's greeting cards, *ochuugen* and *oseibo* gift exchanges, forms of greetings (*aisatsu*), bowing, and many other aspects of everyday Japanese life are all forms of institutionalized politeness. They form much of the structure of everyday life in Japan.

Many of these forms of politeness, however, have been forgotten or are being ignored by contemporary Japanese. I seriously doubt that people are being intentionally rude; rather, I see the decline in such values and rituals as an inevitable consequence of the types of changes that have been occurring in Japanese culture. In particular, I think that the increasing amount of rudeness that we are witness to in our everyday lives—on the trains, in public, and so forth—also reflects the great deal of stress that many Japanese people feel, not only from their normal, everyday activities, but because of the great social and cultural confusion in which they have to live.[23] That is, the cultural changes that we have been discussing, which have essentially led to a cultural duality within a single society, have also produced tension and stress that is felt and acted out by the individuals who live and function within such an environment.

Changes in Japanese culture have also brought with them changes in the nature and meaning of friendship. Traditional collectivistic values meant that one had only a few really good friends but had deep, long-lasting emotional ties to those few friends. Increasing individualism, however, also seems to bring with it larger friendship circles but less intense emotional ties to those friends. If some friendships are cut, others easily replace them. These differences in interpersonal relationships can be witnessed in individualistic and collectivistic societies everywhere (see, for example, Triandis et al. [1988] for more on this topic).

In the San Francisco Bay area, there are many Japanese sojourners and immigrants, especially international students. I know of some cases where young men and women actually form relationships as lovers almost on the basis of convenience in finding a roommate. That is, they agree to become lovers as well as roommates so that they can save on housing costs. When one of them has to go back to Japan, they then break up the relationship. This is a pretty extreme version of relationship formed by convenience and can only occur, to my mind, within a prevailing individualistic value system with a different sense of morality, precisely as we have been discussing.

The nature of family relations has also fundamentally and profoundly changed, especially in terms of parent-child relationships. In my experience, many Japanese youth are growing up today lacking respect for their parents and taking clear advantage of them. They may see their mothers as glorified maids and may even treat them as such. Fathers don't fare much better; many Japanese youth today disrespect or even resent their fathers, who in many cases were absent much of the time when their children were growing up. Thus, children are raised with less basic respect for parents and other family members, and this ultimately spills over into their relationships with all others as adults.

One must keep in mind, though, that this is a two-way street. Children may learn to disrespect their parents and take advantage of them because mothers and fathers alike are not considering carefully the long-term implications of their child-rearing practices.

Not all families are like this, of course. Many fine families in Japan model and teach their children solid values. What I mention here, however, is a growing trend within Japanese society that should be of concern to many. I believe that this trend is a major contributing factor to changes in the psychology of Japanese employees and students, as discussed earlier.

Technology, such as the Walkman, cellular phone, Internet, e-mail, and laptop computers, has contributed greatly to changing Japanese culture and will continue to do so in ways that we cannot imagine now. What we do know is that these devices, while designed for convenience, have created psychological space between people and have meaningful implications for interpersonal relationships in Japanese society. I have traveled to over forty countries, and the fascination with and total reliance (of the Japanese) on the cellular phone is second to none. Such trends cannot occur without social and cultural consequences.

To be sure, some of the changes in Japanese society due to the evolution of cultural duality can be considered good. For example, increasing Japanese individualism is associated with increases in volunteerism. These types of activities are typically found in individualistic cultures, most likely because all people are said to be equal, and as such, we should do what we can to help each other, even perfect strangers. Thus, the increase in volunteerism and concerns about social and individual welfare are in my opinion a direct consequence of increasing Japanese individualism.

Another such example is the increasing focus on care for the elderly, which has become an important issue in Japan because of the large elderly population. Related to this focus is the increasing awareness of the importance of social welfare programs. Many colleges and universities are now geared toward providing education in some aspect of social welfare, and the fact that many students are enrolled in such programs alludes to social trends that I believe are the product of an increasing vision of individualism in Japan.

Another positive consequence of the emerging focus on individualism and individuality is the increased attention given to such social problems as bullying and sexual harassment. In the past these and other social problems were simply ignored and tolerated as part of the "system." With the increasing focus on individual self-worth, such social problems are being tolerated less and less. Bullies are being pursued and reprimanded, and new systems are increasingly being put in place to deal with sexual harassment in universities and businesses around the country. While awareness is still a far cry from that of the United States (which may be at its own extreme in this regard), Japan has progressed in these areas considerably when compared with even a decade ago.

A final example of a positive consequence of Japan's emerging individualism is the increased attention given to individuals with mental health problems such as depression, anxiety disorders, or other social or psychological disorders. In the past these individuals were generally treated as misfits, locked away at home, and basically kept away from the daylight of society. Or they struggled to hide their problems from society when possible. Nowadays, however, there are increased efforts to help these individuals, especially from a psychological viewpoint. These efforts are evident in the increasing number of psychological and counseling clinics in Japan as well as degree programs offered by Japanese universities.

In this chapter I have tried to describe how many of the changes in actual behaviors, interpersonal relationships, and real-life experiences in Japan are directly or indirectly related to the changing Japanese culture and emerging cultural dualities. Taken collectively, they paint a rather different picture of the homogeneous, self-effacing, collectivistic Japanese culture and society than is continually portrayed in the media and by scholars and the lay public alike. Quite frankly, much (not all) of Japanese culture is simply different from what we have been led to believe—or want to believe.

Textnotes

[1] Even the tendency to use last names first in self-identification can be considered a manifestation of this tendency, as it gives primary emphasis to the group to which one belongs (in the case of names, the group is the family).

[2] In fact, in the past, workers who moved from one company to another were often stigmatized as unreliable or untrustworthy.

[3] Of course, I am not saying that all such efforts by leaders and managers in corporate Japan today are viewed as such intrusions. What I am saying, however, is that there is a growing sense of such feelings, and they are likely to grow as Japanese culture continues to change and evolve.

[4] This does not mean that it is nonexistent. I am suggesting that it is less important today than in the past, especially among younger Japanese workers.

[5] That is not to say that leaders of the past did not have similar such characteristics. I think there were many such corporate leaders, including Sony's Akio Morita, for instance. I cite this article here because it is apropos of the time and period.

[6] One may also say that independent thought was punished—*"Deru kugi ha utareru"* (The nail that stands up will be pounded down).

[7] The quality of Japan's education in math and science was once again confirmed by the results of the 1999 Third International Mathematics and Science Study. For more details, see www.timss.org.

8 Of course, part of the boredom problem is the language barrier, as many don't have the language skills to fully understand what is going on in class.

9 I must say, though, that I do not teach full-time at these universities. Instead, I typically teach in intensive courses that are essentially electives; thus, there may be a self-selection process occurring in the classes I teach and in the students to whom I am exposed.

10 http://jin.or.jp/insight

11 I do not have more current data, but I cannot help but think that the trend is similar to that depicted here.

12 http://jin.or.jp/insight

13 Ibid.

14 Ibid.

15 http://www. mext.go.jp

16 One of the most famous individuals in Japanese judo, for example, is Akio Kaminaga. Although he lost the gold medal match in judo in the 1964 Tokyo Olympics to Anton Geesink, the way he lost and the way he carried himself throughout the event and after has made him a legend the world over.

17 I have done judo for thirty-four years, and am a sixth-degree black belt. I have been a former medalist in national competition in the United States and have been a coaching staff member to many international competitions, including two Olympics and three world championships.

18 Differences in national pride between the present and the past in Japan are evident in many Japanese immigrants to the United States. When I speak with some of the older immigrants who live in the U.S., they often tell me that despite the fact that they may have been just average youths in Japan, when they moved to the States they tried hard to succeed in life and "do the right thing" simply "because they

were Japanese." They didn't want others to think badly of all Japanese because of their own shortcomings. That is, they wanted to uphold their nationalistic pride during their sojourn. Younger Japanese immigrants and sojourners to the States, however, have relatively less national pride. Their motivations to excel are often more personal and individualistic. Thus, the data for Japanese judo coaches presented above are commensurate with social changes as a whole.

[19] These outcomes were never studied systematically before in Japanese students of judo because of the lack of psychometrically sound measures of these key psychological concepts. The availability of the ICAPS, however, which was validated with Japanese samples, makes these types of studies possible.

[20] The immense popularity of the sport of judo and of this match in particular can be noted by the fact that, in France, there were more television viewers watching this match alone than watching the opening ceremonies of the Olympic Games. A similar sizable viewer share occurred in Japan as well.

[21] These actions on the part of the Japanese media were aided by a rather one-sided commentary by a member of the Japanese national coaching staff.

[22] For example, take Midori Ito's performance at the 1992 Winter Olympics. Before her last performance, she was told it was impossible for her to get a gold medal. If she skated to a conservative routine, she would easily get a bronze medal. If she skated to a rigorous and more challenging routine, she might get a silver medal. Yet, if she went for the silver but performed poorly, she might not get any medal at all. Nevertheless, she opted to skate her heart out in a difficult routine. That challenge, pride, and determination captured the hearts of many and helped to raise her on a pedestal, despite the fact that she did not get the gold that day.

[23] Not to mention the great pressures felt by the people during uncertain economic times, as when this book was being written.

5

Visions of a New Japan in the Future

Change is inevitable in all societies, and many of the changes we are witness to today in contemporary Japan, for good or bad, are natural and inevitable. They are somewhat akin to similar changes that are occurring, or have occurred, in many other countries and cultures around the world. The changes that are occurring in Japan are unique, however, because they are not simply reflective of the minor changes in lifestyles typically associated with technological progress and modernization in many other societies. Instead, they reflect a major evolution in underlying assumptions, attitudes, beliefs, and value systems—that is, changes in culture. The emerging cultural dualities that we have discussed throughout this book involve newfound heterogeneity, individuality, and dissatisfaction with traditional ways. These changes challenge the essence of Japan in many different ways.

How well is Japan coping with this upheaval? The data I have presented here suggest that Japan as a society and the Japanese as individuals are struggling to find ways to channel their emerging cultural duality into positive outcomes. Thus, there is a lot of room for growth and potential.

One of the reasons the Japanese are struggling is because they, and most students of Japan for that matter, have been slow to recognize that the changes that are occurring are cultural and as such, have not been dealt with head-on. The changes have been slow and silent, beneath conscious awareness, creeping up on Japan until it seems as if everyone woke up one day to a different Japan.

In this final chapter, I offer some visions of a new and different Japan, one that does not throw out the previous, traditional Japan, but instead, one that celebrates the Japan of old within a contemporary and more modern cultural and social framework. As humans, we are uniquely equipped to think about our lives, chart new courses and directions, and take an active role in not only reacting to change, but also predicting and even directing change for the better. I offer this chapter with the assumption that there is a better society not only to which the Japanese can evolve but also one that they can be active participants in molding.

The Cultural Challenge for Corporate Japan

Even though Japan has been busy battling with economic problems for some time and attempting to deal with changing cultural values and attitudes on the part of its workers, even larger challenges lie ahead in the next ten or twenty years because of the cultural duality within the labor force today. One group, generally the older (i.e., over forty years of age), holds more or less to the traditional Japanese values of patience, perseverance, hard work, loyalty to the company, and the like. The second, younger group has a different set of values: merit, individual ability, achievement, and performance. They are also more willing to change jobs and companies to suit their needs.

The challenge to corporate Japan, because of the existence of these two groups, comes largely in the form of labor management and human resources practices. Issues concerning hiring, retention, promotion, evaluation, wages, and even termination are based on a system of rules that are created within a particular cultural framework of fairness. Now comes the difficult part: perceptions of fairness and justice can be, and usually are, very culture-specific.

With essentially two separate cultural groups now making up the labor force, however, one of the major challenges is that what is considered fair for one group is not necessarily fair for the other. Thus, while promotion and wage increases based on seniority may be perceived as fair by the older, traditional Japanese, it will not be perceived that way by the younger, more individualistic and merit-driven employees. When such human resources systems are perceived as *un*fair, feelings of loyalty, commitment, and trust decline, which is what we are observing today.

Many of the feelings and reactions I have observed among the Japanese labor force in relation to changing personnel systems, especially in terms of the decline in lifetime employment and the institution of merit-based performance, remind me of what happened during the days of glasnost and perestroika in the former Soviet Union. These changes, brought about essentially for sociopolitical and economic reasons, were also fueled by a changing youth culture that questioned the traditional ways of Marx. Many of the older generation, however, lamented Russia's conversion from a socialist to a capitalist society. They were very worried about their futures. As many told me, communism and socialism may not have been the best political and economic systems in the world, but at least there was stability; they knew where they were and where they would be in the future, and they could count on stability in their homes and lives. But, with the introduction of glasnost and perestroika, their futures were shaky, society was turned upside down, and the younger and older generations were at odds with each other. While the social changes in Russia may have been perceived as essentially good by many outsiders, to those middle-aged and older individuals who had given their lives to the system and who had trusted the system to take care of them in their later years, the changing society and culture brought only worry and apprehension.[1]

The problem that faces corporate Japan today is how to create a system of personnel/labor management that can be perceived simultaneously as fair to both cultural groups that form its workforce. While such a goal may seem unlikely to many, the approach to this issue need not be a mutually exclusive dichotomy. There are many ways for corporate Japan to react to the country's evolving culture and to create new systems of labor management, ones that essentially incorporate multiple cultural value systems to develop a collectively fair system of hiring, promotion, and termination. Such a view may require the creation of individualized systems of hiring, retention, pay, and promotion that are commensurate with multiple cultural expectations of fairness.

What makes dealing with these issues particularly difficult is the existence of the stressful and tense environment in which individuals and employees must function effectively. Thus, not only is there stress placed on the employees because of the necessity to be productive and competitive within a global or domestic market economy; there is the additional stress placed on individual employees by the dual cultural system within which they must operate. This undoubtedly makes corporate life in Japan especially difficult during these trying times and creates an extra burden for corporations and top-level executives in designing ways to effectively deal with these challenges.

One key to Japan's future prosperity is not necessarily how it deals with the cultural needs it has right now; rather, it is whether Japanese companies can create a system of organizational culture and climate that is flexible enough to flow with the continuing evolution of Japanese culture over the next several decades. That is, instead of merely *reacting* to the current situation, corporate Japan must begin to consider how it can *proactively influence* cultural changes in the future. Some of these changes will involve the transition from the traditional total quality management systems that Japan has become famous for to what is known as learning and world-class organizations in organizational and business literature. Japanese companies need to move from essentially a passive role in social change to an active one in guiding and easing this and other transitions.

The Japanese corporate world must begin to recognize the enormous role it plays as an agent for change in shaping Japanese culture. Corporations are, after all, the end point of the major goal of education. In a broad sense, therefore, many of the skills emphasized by the educational system are dictated by corporate Japan's requirements for effective operation. If corporate Japan chooses to recruit, hire, and retain individuals with certain sets of skills, then the educational system will necessarily react accordingly. In this fashion, corporate Japan, as a proactive agent, will effect social and cultural change.[2]

What I mentioned earlier bears repeating: the labor force may essentially represent a cultural duality right now, but in twenty to thirty years, the individuals constituting the younger generations now will have become the older generation, and a new young generation will take its place. In other words in one generation's time, corporate Japan will be looking at an entirely different type of individual to become the mainstay of the labor force. It is at this crucial point in time, then, that the Japanese business sector has the chance to influence that future generation; the opportunity won't be available later.

Where to begin? Although I may not have the answers, I do know where corporate Japan can start to search for solutions. Fairness and justice, for instance, are well-studied topics in social psychology, not only within the United States but across many countries and cultures. The information from that body of knowledge needs to be brought to the attention of businesspersons in corporate Japan who can review and evaluate existing human resources practices and design creative new policies and practices for the present and for the future. At the same time, research on organizational culture and companies as change agents of society needs to be brought to bear. Other sources of necessary information may also exist. The right mix of people with the appropriate information needs to be assembled for creative brainstorming about solutions that are specific to the Japanese. Informed decisions, not guesses or best approximations, are the key.

The Cultural Challenge for the Japanese Educational System

Although there is no doubt in my mind that Japan's educational system has met well the needs of society to produce citizens of the recent past, we know from our discussion in chapter 4 that today's and tomorrow's needs require creative change within the educational sector. In this section of the chapter, I develop four areas of consideration that are directly related to Japan's evolving need for changes within the educational system.

First, English training must shift from an emphasis on reading and writing to conversation. Most Japanese students learn some English during their junior high and high school years, and while most can read and write English, they cannot speak it very well. Limited oral English skills mean limited conversational skills. Given that conversational English is clearly the language of the next century, if the Japanese are to be well prepared to contribute to world affairs, they must be able to communicate well with others who speak English.[3]

Second, the Japanese educational system needs to examine how well it is training its students in international and intercultural adaptability. In the United States, living effectively in a multicultural environment is a major topic in education, from elementary through university. This emphasis on multicultural education is no doubt a reflection of the growing recognition of the diversity of the world in which we live and of the importance of gaining some basic skills in order to function effectively within that diversity. In Japan, however, most intercultural training is simply language training, and more specifically, English language training. But research has demonstrated convincingly that language skills alone are not sufficient to ensure intercultural sensitivity. What is necessary is the development of a core set of psychological skills that enable us to live flexibly and effectively in a dynamic, multicultural environment (for more information, see Matsumoto [1999b]). Language training without accompanying cultural competence training can amount to nothing more than equipping speakers to offend others faster, a current problem among many Japanese who speak English without cultural awareness.

In fact, in the book cited above, I report research using the ICAPS (described in chapter 4) in large samples of American and Japanese university students. As I explained there, the ICAPS assesses the four key psychological skills I believe are important to function effectively in a multicultural environment—emotion regulation, openness, flexibility, and autonomy. Our studies have indicated quite convincingly that Japanese university students have considerably lower ICAPS scores than do American students.[4] Thus, while it is apparent that the Japanese educational system may produce students who undoubtedly have superior math and science abilities, such skills may be gained at the sacrifice of the interpersonal and intercultural skills that are necessary for life in the new millennium. This finding may also explain why Japanese society is having such a difficult time dealing with emerging cultural dualities—because its individuals are not psychologically prepared to handle the stress inherent in an environment of diversity. If this is the case, it suggests that the Japanese educational system reexamine its priorities and, as described above, consider the improvement of such intercultural skills as part of its educational curricula. The development of these skills will undoubtedly aid in the development of other values that are important in our increasingly pluralistic world, such as tolerance for diversity, respect for others, conflict resolution skills, and the like.

Third, the Japanese educational system needs to reexamine its emphasis on rote memorization and the learning of facts. In my experience the typical Japanese student excels at learning facts and figures and at performing other academic tasks that essentially require patience, perseverance, and effort. What many Japanese students lack is the ability to think about problems creatively, critically, and autonomously.[5] The single-minded focus on entrance examinations, which by their very nature are tests of memory, has essentially brought about a culture of "memory robots" who excel at memorizing information, but who have difficulty in thinking creatively about the world around them. They are good (perhaps some of the best in the world) at memorizing all the facts about anything, through the sheer amount of time and effort placed on the memorization process.

In my experience these memory robots are not solely a consequence of the educational system; it seems that the response of many Japanese individuals in leadership positions to calls for improvement or change is *simply to do more of the same thing they have been doing for years*. The response of many teachers, then, is to require students to learn more by studying more and memorizing more, thus producing memory robots.[6] The response of many sports coaches to the challenge of domestic and international competition is similar—to require athletes to train longer and harder doing generally the same things they have been doing. In addition the response of many managers in corporate Japan is also to have their employees produce more by working longer and harder at performing essentially the same tasks in the same manner as they have been doing. Thus, the robots I refer to here do not exist solely because of the educational system but because such behavior is encouraged in many arenas of life.

Years and years of this reinforcement can essentially stifle creativity, which is a major problem facing Japan today.[7] This is a serious limitation, because as a result many Japanese students cannot get outside their "cultural box" to think about the world in new ways.

Creativity and critical thinking are essential ingredients to being successful, competitive, and effective citizens of tomorrow's world.

Finally, Japanese teacher training institutions need to add to their curriculum the study of theory and methodology that teachers can use to develop in their students some of the skills and values that I have been discussing, and that are important to living in the twenty-first century. In many classrooms in Japan today, for example, teachers still practice the passive learning approach, where students all sit facing the teacher, who lectures uninterrupted for an entire class period. One particular corollary of this approach is the dominance and omnipotence that is associated with the role of the teacher. I know of many instances where teachers get quite upset when students merely raise their hands to ask questions or, heaven forbid, challenge what the teacher may be saying. Such teaching methods inevitably lead to a stifling of creativity and independent, critical thinking. The physical layout of the learning environment is also designed to meet the needs of yesterday's Japan, not today's—and especially not tomorrow's.

The Cultural Challenge for Japanese Sports

In this section, while I direct my comments to the sport I know best, judo, I cannot help but think that much of what I discuss here should be applicable to other sports and cultural activities as well. All sports, especially those considered in the physical education curricula of schools, colleges, and universities, most likely need to deal with the issues described below in some way, shape, or form.[8]

The emergence of cultural dualities in Japan has essentially created a dichotomy in Japanese judo. On the one hand judo is a sport. This is the view of the younger generations, who generally see judo in light of the Olympic Games and other high-level competitions, and of many coaches. In this view of judo, like any other sport, the goal of practice is to win at competition. One's worth as an athlete, coach, or administrator is determined in large part by the success of one's team in competition.

On the other hand, many others, especially the older generations, see judo as a martial art, a way of life, a method for teaching moral values and virtues to young people and for developing responsible citizens. Competition is not considered to be necessary or important, and neither is winning. What is important is character development.

There is a major rift between these two groups, as I would imagine there is in many types of cultural or sporting activities in Japan. The mass media have blatantly promoted the win-lose perspective. Among all Olympic sports, judo garners more medals for Japan than any other category, and the media swarm around the athletes, bringing an incredible amount of publicity, public relations attention, and many other benefits to the judo organization. Winning medals also has important economic ramifications behind the scenes, as funds from the Japanese Olympic Committee (JOC) are granted to the All Japan Judo Federation in large part based on medals won. The more medals, the more money. (This is, in fact, not unique to Japan.) More money means greater resources for training that will ensure future success. This cycle results in an almost exclusive focus on training to win, at the sacrifice of personal character development and the attainment of moral virtues. Enormous pressure is brought to bear on the coaches, then the athletes, not only by the organization but by society as well.[9]

The rift is widened still further because of the sociopolitical nature of sports administration. Inevitably, because of the emphasis on winning medals in competition, individuals who harbor similar goals and values (i.e., of winning) are drawn to administrative involvement. Those are the people who are elected or appointed to important positions in sports administration. Others who feel and think differently either do not have the power to say anything or are left outside the system entirely. Those who "rock the boat," that is, expound values or a philosophy that may be contrary to the prevalent competitive views, may be cast aside, isolated, and/or discriminated against in many ways.

These differing philosophies about the nature, role, function, and goals of judo are at least partially rooted in the cultural duality that exists in Japan today. Views of judo as primarily a sport, with its emphasis on individual achievement, are rooted in the growing sense of individuality and autonomy that has infiltrated mainstream Japanese youth culture and originally got its start during the American occupation following World War II. It makes sense, in fact, that in order to aspire to the highest levels of sports competition, such as the World Championships or Olympic Games, one must necessarily be individualistic and selfish in one's focus, because such achievements require tremendous amounts of self-determination and motivation. Views of judo primarily as a system of intellectual, moral, or physical education are rooted in the culture that characterized previous, stereotypic notions of Japan.

The challenge for the Japanese judo world of the future, therefore, is to bring these two groups of people—or more importantly, these two different philosophies—together so that they may exist simultaneously and complement each other. How can this be done? First of all, one would have to start with the vision that individual achievement at the highest levels need not require the sacrifice of the development of moral values and virtues. The degree to which such a vision can be shared by athletes, coaches, administrators, the media, and the general public will enable these groups to come together to redefine the meaning of sports, competition, and training in the original spirit of the Olympic movement.

Second, at least in the case of judo, an organizational structure within Japan (and elsewhere) that allows for the dual monitoring and administration of both philosophies is already in place: the JOC. Within this body are national federations of the various sports. In Japan, for example, judo is represented by the All Japan Judo Federation. It is only natural and proper, therefore, for all sports-related matters of judo competition in Japan to be regulated by the All Japan Judo Federation. In Japan, however, there is yet another organization—the Kodokan—which, as the founder of judo in the world, is considered the "mecca" of judo. It could well serve as the moral light of judo in Japan, and in the entire world, creating and administering programs of moral, intellectual, and physical education all over the world. This program, then, could complement the activities of the bodies that regulate sport judo.

These potential developments depend on the ability of leaders in judo in Japan to recognize the major problems and challenges facing the discipline and to envision solutions to these problems. Society as a whole also plays a major role in promoting the image of athletes. We all like winners, and we have honored and glorified champions in many different ways. I am not saying that we necessarily downplay this attitude, but I am suggesting that we open our minds to a larger definition of *winning*. Winning in a sports competition can be a glorious achievement and should rightfully be praised. Yet winning at life and being a citizen of strong character is also a glorious achievement that deserves its fair share of recognition.

Transforming Japanese Culture
in the Future

One of the challenges that lies ahead for Japan regarding its emerging individualism is how to channel and transform it in such a manner as to lead to less stressful, more productive, and happier lives. The increasing individualism and other changes in Japanese culture are not themselves problematic; they are natural and inevitable reactions to changes in the environment within which we live, brought about by technology, affluence, changing demographics, and the like. These cultural adjustments are Japan's reaction to its changing world and, as such, should be guided, not suppressed.

Let's first pause to consider the nature of Japan's individualism. Many people believe that it is an attempt to become more American. That is, because Americans are stereotypically considered to be individualistic, I think that many Japanese believe they are adopting American individualism. Many people, in fact, attribute Japan's growing individualism directly to the United States.

Such a view is not entirely incorrect, especially when one considers that many of the educational, business, political, and structural reforms of Japan after the war were instituted by Americans, most notably by General Douglas MacArthur. In many senses, therefore, the social and cultural changes we are witnessing today may in fact be a direct consequence of the reforms that MacArthur instituted in postwar Japan, especially those in education.

Quite frankly, though, Japanese individuality cannot be American individualism.[10] It makes no more sense to transplant American individualistic values and customs to Japan and expect them to grow in a similar manner than it does to borrow Japanese management practices at Toyota and simply apply them to American auto manufacturers. Replanting one cultural system in other cultural soil doesn't work. Cultural traits work in their original culture precisely because of the larger environmental context in which they exist. That is, American individualism works in the United States because of the country's geography, resources, languages, history, and a host of other factors. Transferring such values to the Japanese context will not create another America. Instead, what results is a unique form of Japanese individualism that is clearly perceived as antithetical to the mainstream culture.

Japanese individuality is clearly not American individualism. What we have in Japan is almost a rejection of traditional Japanese values, which is mislabeled individualism or "the American way" by many in Japan. Japanese individuality is unique; it is a seemingly dichotomous reaction to traditional Japanese collectivism, individuality that exists within a greater collectivistic society.

How can this unique form of individualism be channeled into positive outcomes? I believe the future of Japan partially rests on its ability to create an *in-*

dividualistic collectivism that represents a rapproche-
ment of two opposing cultural dimensions, a culture
that enjoys and celebrates individuality and diversity
and at the same time recognizes the pursuit of group
and collective goals. It would be a culture that recovers
and celebrates the cultural values and perspectives that
have made Japan unique for centuries, but that also
finds new ways of reframing and expressing them.[11]

And what might this individualistic collectivism look
like? It is a cultural rubric that has at its core the basic
collectivist values and virtues that Japan has come to
be known for across the centuries: perseverance, loyalty, commitment, dedication, harmony, self-discipline,
and the like. Add to these Japan's emphasis on
ingroups, social stratification, and hierarchies, and we
have the bedrock of traditional Japanese culture upon
which aspects of individualism can be added.

Contemporary and future Japan may come to see
the myriad ways in which these values may be expressed with an overlay of individualistic traits that
operate at the level of the person. An example may
help here. Certain actions, for instance, the bow, became synonymous with particular values (e.g., respect);
the lack of such actions symbolized the nonexistence
of that value. In the future, individualized collectivism
may mean that the core Japanese values may be expressed not in one, but in two, three, a hundred, or a
thousand ways, *depending on the individual.* That is,
individuals may develop their own unique ways of
holding and expressing these core values. Thus, what

context?

may become institutionalized or ritualized is not necessarily the age-old actions that have traditionally expressed a core value, but tolerance and reinforcement
of unique ways in which individuals can express them.

Individualized collectivism is a concept that suggests that a society can celebrate cultural diversity in
thought or action (individuality) while maintaining core
values related to the importance of group and hierarchy (collectivism). I do believe it is important for Japan
to maintain its basic core values, those that have come
to represent the essence of Japanese culture. There is
no reason to "throw out the (so-called) baby with the
bath water," nor should people fear that traditional
aspects of Japanese society will be lost. Instead, Japan needs to find ways in which its basic essence can
be celebrated in different and unique ways by its
people. Achieving such a goal will require coordination, in a sense, among parents, educational systems
and agents, corporate Japan, the political infrastructure, and the like. Yet, it can be achieved.

Challenges for the Future

Technological advances promise to continue to influence culture and society for years to come. We have
learned to graft cartilage in a damaged knee. Medical
scientists have reproduced brain cells in monkeys. We
can keep people physically alive today longer than ever
before. We can grow test-tube babies. We have im-
planted artificial hearts. One day we may be able to

prolong life beyond our wildest dreams, and even bring about death in a quick and painless manner.

As technology advances, however, complex questions about morality and ethics that we have never even dreamed of arise, along with new moral dilemmas and challenges that we will need to face. Future technological developments in weapons and communications technologies will also bring their own moral and ethical dilemmas. Friendships, work and status relationships, and family ties will all be different. People will have new ways of thinking about themselves, their loved ones, and their futures. With such great changes occurring, how can everyday life not be fundamentally influenced by technology?

I believe that many Japanese individuals recognize that many challenges will face them in the future. Because of this growing awareness of the need for a reexamination of social and cultural values, many Japanese are refocusing their energies on new and better outcomes, challenging their previous beliefs and their own stereotypes of the world.

In any capitalistic society, it is a truism that money is supposed to be able to buy happiness (although one may not readily admit it). And to a certain degree, people believe this to be true. In all of the opinion polls conducted by the government and by private agencies, for example, life satisfaction is always highly correlated with family income. That is, the more money available, the happier a person is in general. In these same surveys, job satisfaction is also always positively correlated with income. That is, as your pay increases, so does your satisfaction with your job.

Of course, these associations are never perfect, which is why I believe that money can buy a certain amount of happiness, but not all.[12] In fact, many Japanese individuals are beginning to reexamine the role of materialism in terms of what is really important in their lives. In a survey by *Asahi Shimbun* (1998, 11 March), for example, comparing responses from 1985 with those from 1998, a substantially smaller percentage of individuals believed that almost anything enjoyable can be obtained with money (Figure 5.1).

Figure 5.1
Can You Get Almost Anything Enjoyable with Money?

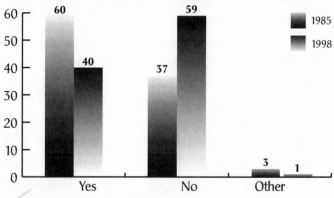

These figures tell me that Japan may be on the rebound from the decadence of materialism that may have characterized it prior to 1985. Just as many scholars believe the United States is experiencing a turnaround in its social and cultural values, becoming more conservative and rebounding from a few decades of materialistic decadence, Japan appears to be doing the same.

In fact, more recent polls[13] indicate that the number of people who believe that more attention should be paid to the welfare of the nation and of society, instead of focusing on personal fulfillment, is on the rise (see Figure 5.2 in the Appendix).

Another sign of positive change is that Japan's Ministry of Education, Culture, Sports, Science, and Technology has unveiled its "Educational Reform Plan for the Twenty-first Century," which calls for education reform and the revitalization of schools, families, and communities.[14] These reforms center around seven core goals:

1. Improve students' basic scholastic proficiency in easy-to-understand classes
2. Encourage youth to become open and warmhearted adults through participating in community services and various programs
3. Change learning environments to those that are enjoyable and free of worries
4. Make schools that parents and communities can trust
5. Train teachers as real professionals of education
6. Promote the establishment of universities that meet international standards
7. Establish an educational philosophy suitable for the new century and improve the provision for education

It is no coincidence that the Ministry of Education's

reform plan touches on many of the issues we have discussed in this book, particularly those earlier in this chapter on the cultural challenges for the educational system. Nurturing youth into becoming "open" and "warmhearted" citizens speaks to many of the issues concerning values and moral virtues we have discussed, as does internationalizing and modernizing education. Of course, the future will be the judge as to whether such reform plans are merely lip service or meaningful plans of action with significant consequences.[15] The fact that such reform is discussed and implemented is at least a step in the right direction.

These data and the growing voice of many concerned Japanese citizens whom I meet professionally through my research and teaching or personally in my travels suggest that in fact Japan may well be on the road toward self-evaluation of its social and cultural values and toward redirecting them to a collectively more functional and effective set of beliefs and behaviors than exists today.

As Japan looks to the future, all agents of society—parents, families, teachers, and co-workers as well as institutions, organizations, companies, and the like—will need to come together to develop an outlook for the future that holds true to those values, attitudes, beliefs, and behaviors that define us not only as essentially Japanese but also as essentially human. We should define those values and not have them defined for us by technology, money, changing demographic situations, or our own apathy or ignorance. I am not one to tell any individual, let alone a nation, what those values should be. They become, I believe, self-evident as long as we engage in the process of actively and deliberately thinking about and choosing them for ourselves and teaching them to our children. If we don't take such a proactive role, we run the risk of losing our human essence—what makes us fundamentally and profoundly different from all other animals. If we have the courage to choose our moral values and actively teach them to our children, then we will be able to live more enlightened lives. Japan, it seems to me, is at the brink of once again leading the world in teaching the rest of us what it means to be human, through navigating the challenges posed by its newfound heterogeneity and dualistic cultural identity. Effectively dealing with its emerging cultural dualism in what was once a more homogeneous, unicultural society, may be Japan's biggest challenge, and contribution to its legacy, for generations to come.

Textnotes

1 Japan's situation is not totally akin to Russia's, in that Japan has much of the corporate infrastructure and resources, including capital and cultural resources, with which to address its needs and challenges. Thus, while Russia continues to struggle today economically, Japan has the potential to fare much better in dealing with the cultural changes because of its economic position.

2 Of course, it is not easy to achieve these goals. Witness the difficulties many Japanese companies have had in adapting to new styles of thought and action after they merged

with European or American companies, such as Nissan and Renault.

3 Some people may suggest that I am an ethnocentric American who doesn't see a similar need for the United States, and who believes that the world should accommodate to Americans' convenience. I do not believe that; I also believe that it is important for Americans, who are perhaps the most monolingual, monocultural people of the world, to gain language (and more importantly, cultural) competence in a language other than English.

4 Some critics may suggest that it is only natural that Americans score higher on this test than do the Japanese because an American created the test. But remember that the test was originally developed by and validated on Japanese samples, not American.

5 This is also related to their lower ICAPS scores described above, which are likely a product of the overemphasis on rote memorization.

6 The fact of the matter is that the current elementary and junior high school situation has changed so much that teachers often can't control what goes on in class.

7 The problem is exacerbated because, as I have suggested elsewhere, I believe that contemporary Japanese youth *want* to be creative because of their newfound individuality.

8 In fact I am absolutely convinced that the issues should be the same, because the original intent of sporting activities as part of physical education was to complement intellectual education in the classroom by providing moral and physical lessons outside the class. It seems to me that many sports, not only judo, in the physical education curricula in schools have lost this original objective.

9 I do not underestimate the effects of the American occupation of Japan after World War II on this view of judo. After the war, judo was initially banned by the occupation

forces, only to be resurrected a few years later, but only as a sport, not as a martial art. Thus, the almost exclusive focus of judo as a sport can be seen as having its roots during the American occupation. Judo's emergence in the Olympics in 1964 continued to foster this view thereafter.

10 To me, American individualism, revolving around self-reliance and freedom, symbolizes four key concepts: equality, choice, personal responsibility, and commitment. Equality is a cornerstone value that ensures that people treat others with kindness, consideration, and sincerity, in the hope that others will treat them in the same fashion. Individual choice means that people have the ability to choose what path in life is right for them, their friends, their families, their careers, their dreams, and their goals. Taking responsibility means that individuals accept the obligations and duties that are associated with the choices they make in their lives, whether good or bad, right or wrong, and that once choices are made, individuals assume the personal responsibility to put out the effort that is required to make their choices come true. Finally, American individualism includes a good deal of commitment to home, church, and community, for which they have held much respect. Traditional Americans have been devoted and committed to their homes and families, to their religious and spiritual lives, and to the communities in which they have lived. They have worked together, played together, and genuinely cared for the people in those three groups. American individualism, therefore, is not a rejection of all others; instead, it is a symbol of a balance of individual uniqueness and collectivistic concerns.

11 You may notice the deliberate use of *individuality* in the context of Japan and *individualism* in reference to the United States. These terms are not identical. Edward Stewart and Milton Bennett make a distinction between the two terms (1991). My understanding of the difference concerns

the unit of analysis. Individuality refers to the fact that individuals within any society or culture may have strong or unique personal characteristics that make them stand out within their social context. Certainly, individuality can occur within any sociocultural context, whether individualistic, collectivistic, or otherwise. Individualism, however, refers to a system that exists on the social and cultural levels, that is certainly witnessed in individuals but clearly exists in other strata of society as well (e.g., family, business practices and procedures, government, laws, etc.). In text, I refer to the creation of an individualistic collectivism as a social system, which is broader than Stewart and Bennett's concept of individuality but not as encompassing as individualism.

12 Also consider the data on national income and life satisfaction presented in chapter 1.

13 See, for example, the 1999 Opinion Survey on Social Consciousness from the public relations office of the prime minister, 1-6-1 Nagata Cho, Chiyoda-Ku, Tokyo, 100–8914.

14 see www.mext.go.jp

15 These new goals of educational reform have been announced. The issue now is to implement reform. But change will not be easy, especially because the real power in the educational system is in the hands of the "old boy" network. To the advantage of this group, the law often prohibits its members' removal from positions of power, making educational reform difficult and slow.

Appendix

Figure 1.2
Attitudes of Japanese and Finnish Youth
toward the Future (page 23 of text)

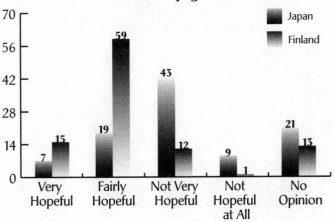

Figure 2.1
Collectivism Data* (page 41 of text)

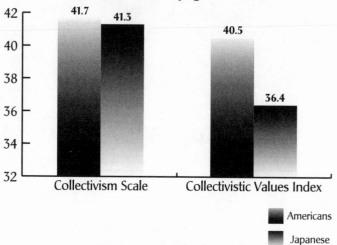

Americans
Japanese

Figure 2.2
Collectivism Study† (page 41 of text)

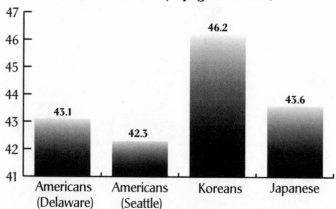

* from Carter and Dinnel 1997
† from Yamaguchi et al. 1995

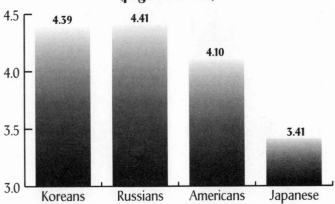

Figure 2.3
Collectivism Scores toward Families in Four Countries
(page 42 of text)

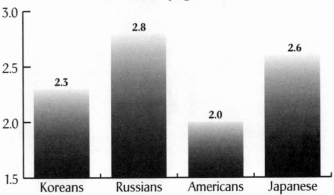

Figure 2.4
Collectivism Scores toward Strangers in
Four Countries (page 44 of text)

Figure 2.9
U.S.-Japan Differences in Self-Concept[‡]
(page 52 of text)

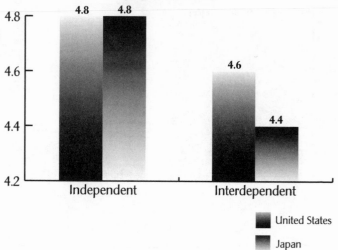

Figure 2.13
Determiners of Salary and Position in Japan
(page 71 of text)

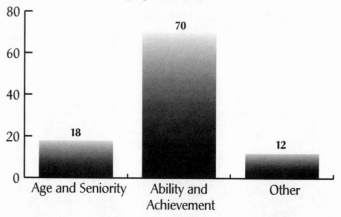

[‡] from Kleinknecht et al. 1997

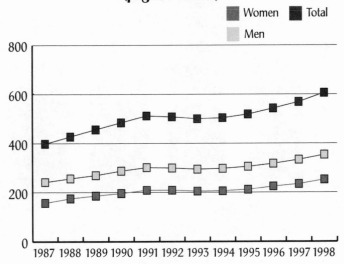

Figure 2.16
Number of People Wishing to Change Jobs
(page 77 of text)

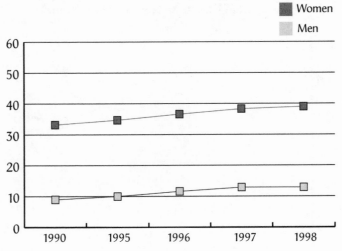

Figure 2.17
Number of Part-Time Workers (page 77 of text)

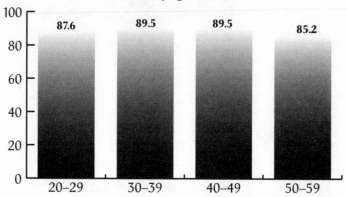

Figure 3.2
Percentage Who Believe Youth Lack Morals and
Social Skills (page 110 of text)

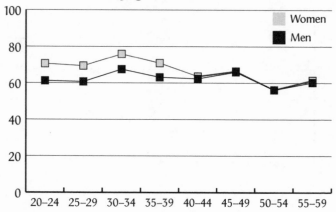

Figure 4.1
Does Sexual Discrimination Exist in Japan?
(page 143 of text)

Figure 5.2
Where Should More Attention Be Paid?
(page 201 of text)

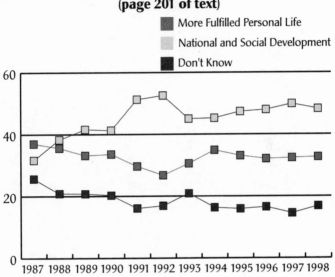

References

Arikawa, Hiroko, and Donald I. Templer. 1998. "Comparison of Japanese and American College Students on Collectivism and Social Context of Decision Making." *Psychological Reports* 83, 577–78.

Barry, Herbert. 1980. "Description and Uses of the Human Relations Area Files." In *Handbook of Cross-Cultural Psychology. Vol. 2: Methodology*, edited by Harry C. Triandis. Boston: Allyn and Bacon.

Befu, Harumi. 1986. "The Social and Cultural Background of Child Development in Japan and the United States." In *Child Development and Education in Japan*, edited by Harold Stevenson, Hiroshi Azuma, and Kenji Hakuta, 13–27. New York: W. H. Freeman.

Benedict, Ruth. 1946. *The Chrysanthemum and the Sword: Patterns of Japanese Culture*. New York: Houghton Mifflin and Company.

Berry, John, W. H. Poortinga, Marshall H. Segall, and Pierre R. Dasen. 1992. *Cross-Cultural Psychology: Re-*

search and Applications. New York: Cambridge University Press.

Carter, Kim, and Dale Dinnel. 1997. "Conceptualization of Self-Esteem in Collectivistic and Individualistic Cultures." Paper presented at the Western Psychological Association.

Diener, Ed, and Shigehiro Oishi. 2000. "Money and Happiness: Income and Subjective Well-Being across Nations." In *Culture and Subjective Well-Being*, edited by Ed Diener and Shigehiro Oishi, 185–218. Cambridge, MA: MIT Press.

Dinnel, Dale. 2001. "Culture and Self: A Reconceptualization of the Role of Individualism and Collectivism." Paper presented at a conference in Bath, NSW, Australia.

Doi, Takeo. 1973. *The Anatomy of Dependence*. Tokyo: Kodansha International.

Dore, Ronald. 1958. *City Life in Japan: A Study of a Tokyo Ward*. Berkeley: University of California Press.

Earley, P. Christopher. 1989. "Social Loafing and Collectivism: A Comparison of the United States and the People's Republic of China." *Administrative Science Quarterly* 34, 565–81.

Ekman, Paul. 1972. "Universal and Cultural Differences in Facial Expression of Emotion." In *Nebraska Symposium on Motivation, 1971*, edited by J. R. Cole, 207–83. Lincoln: Nebraska University Press.

Ekman, Paul, and Wallace Friesen. 1969. "The Repertoire of Nonverbal Behavior: Categories, Origins, Usage, and Coding." *Semiotica* 1, 49–98.

Friesen, Wallace V. 1972. "Cultural Differences in Facial Expressions in a Social Situation: An Experimental Test of the Concept of Display Rules." Dissertation, University of California, San Francisco.

Gabrenya, William K., Y. Wang, and B. Latane. 1985. "Social Loafing on an Optimizing Task: Cross-Cultural Differences among Chinese and Americans." *Journal of Cross-Cultural Psychology* 16, 223–42.

Gudykunst, William B., G. Gao, K. L. Schmidt, and T. Nishida. 1992. "The Influence of Individualism-Collectivism, Self-Monitoring, and Predicted-Outcome Value on Communication in Ingroup and Outgroup Relationships." *Journal of Cross-Cultural Psychology* 23, 196–213.

Hall, John. 1968. *Japan: From Prehistory to Modern Times*. New York: Dell Publishing.

Hall, John, and Marius Jansen. 1968. *Studies in the Institutional History of Early Modern Japan*. Princeton: Princeton University Press.

Hearn, Lafcadio. 1894. *Glimpses of Unfamiliar Japan*. Reprint, Tokyo: Charles E. Tuttle, 1976.

Hofstede, Geert H. 1984. *Culture's Consequences: International Differences in Work-Related Values*, abridged ed. Beverly Hills: Sage Publications.

———. 1980. *Culture's Consequences: International Differences in Work-Related Values*. Beverly Hills: Sage Publications.

Ishihara, Shintaro. 1989. *The Japan that Can Say No*. New York: Simon and Schuster.

Japan Times. 2001. "Perverse Individualist Embraces Opportunity Where Others See Gloom." 11 March, 1.

Kashima, Yoshihisa, Susumu Yamaguchi, Uichol Kim, and S. C. Choi. 1995. "Culture, Gender, and Self: A Perspective from Individualism-Collectivism Research." *Journal of Personality and Social Psychology* 69, 925–37.

Kim, Min-Sun, J. E. Hunter, A. Miyahara, A. M. Horvath, M. Bresnahan, and H. J. Yoon. 1996. "Individual versus Culture-Level Dimensions of Individualism and Collectivism: Effects on Preferred Conversation Styles." *Communication Monographs* 63, 29–49.

Kleinknecht, Ronald A., Dale Dinnel, Erica E. Kleinknecht, Natsuki Hiruma, and N. Harada. 1997. "Cultural Factors in Social Anxiety: A Comparison of Social Phobia Symptoms and Taijin Kyofusho." *Journal of Anxiety Disorders* 11, 157–77.

Kroeber, Alfred Lairs, and Clyde Kluckhohn. 1952. *Culture: A Critical Review of Concepts and Definitions*. Cambridge, MA: Peabody Museum.

Latane, B. 1981. "The Psychology of Social Impact." *American Psychologist* 36, 343–56.

Latane, Bibb, K. Williams, and S. Harkins. 1979. "Many Hands Make Light the Work: The Causes and Consequences of Social Loafing." *Journal of Personality and Social Psychology* 37, 322–32.

Lee, Minjoo. 1995. "Differences between Americans, Koreans and Korean Americans on Individualism and Collectivism." Thesis, San Francisco State University.

Markus, Hazel R., and Shinobu Kitayama. 1991. "Culture and the Self: Implications for Cognition, Emotion, and Motivation." *Psychological Review* 98, no. 2, 224–53.

Matsumoto, David. 1999a. "Culture and Self: An Empirical Assessment of Markus and Kitayama's Theory of Independent and Interdependent Self-Construals." *Asian Journal of Social Psychology* 2, 289–310.

———. 1999b. *Nihonjin no kokusai tekiouryoku*. Tokyo: Honno Tomosha.

———. 1990. "Cultural Similarities and Differences in Display Rules." *Motivation and Emotion* 14, no. 3, 195–214.

Matsumoto, David, Theodora Consolacion, Hiroshi Yamada, Ryuta Suzuki, Brenda Franklin, Sunita Paul, Rebecca Ray, and Hideko Uchida. In press. "American-Japanese Cultural Differences in Judgments of Emotional Expressions of Different Intensities. *Cognition and Emotion*.

Matsumoto, David, Hokao Takeuchi, and Kenji Horiyama. 2001. "Cultural Differences in the Values of Judo Instructors." *Budagaku Kenkyu* 34, no. 1, 1–10.

Matsumoto, David, Fazilet Kasri, and Kristie Kooken. 1999. "American-Japanese Cultural Differences in Judgments of Expression Intensity and Subjective Experience. *Cognition and Emotion* 13, 201–18.

Matsumoto, David, Fazilet Kasri, Erin Milligan, Usha Singh, and Jenny The. 1997a. "Lay Conceptions of Culture: Do Students and Researchers Understand Culture in the Same Way?" Unpublished manuscript.

Matsumoto, David, Michelle Weissman, Ken Preston, Bonny Brown, and Cenita Kupperbusch. 1997b. "Context-Specific Measurement of Individualism-Collectivism on the Individual Level: The IC Interpersonal Assessment Inventory (ICIAI)." *Journal of Cross-Cultural Psychology* 28, 743–67.

Matsumoto, David, and Debora Fletcher. 1996. "Cultural Influences on Disease." *Journal of Gender, Culture, and Health* 1, 71–82.

Matsumoto, David, Tsutomu Kudoh, and Sachiko Takeuchi. 1996. "Changing Patterns of Individualism and Collectivism in the United States and Japan." *Culture and Psychology* 2, 77–107.

Minami, Hiroshi. 1970. *Psychology of the Japanese People.* Honolulu: East-West Center.

Misumi, Jyuji, and M. F. Peterson. 1987. "Supervision and Leadership." In *Advances in Organizational Psychology: An International Review,* edited by Bernard M. Bass, Peter J. D. Drenth, and Peter Weissenberg, 220–31. Newbury Park, CA: Sage Publications.

———. 1985. *The Behavioral Science of Leadership: An Interdisciplinary Japanese Research Program.* Ann Arbor: University of Michigan Press.

Moeran, Brian. 1986. "Individual, Group, and Seishin:

Japan's Internal Cultural Debate." In *Japanese Culture and Behavior: Selected Readings*, edited by Takie S. Lebra and William P. Lebra, 62–79. Honolulu: University of Hawaii Press.

Morris, Ivan. 1975. *The Nobility of Failure: Tragic Heroes in the History of Japan*. New York: Holt Rinehart and Winston.

Murdock, George P., Clellan S. Ford, and Alfred E. Hudson. 1971. *Outline of Cultural Materials*. New Haven, CT: Human Relations Area Files.

Nakane, Chie. 1997. "Japanese Culture within International Society." In *Japan as I See It*, edited by NHK Overseas Broadcasting Department, 179–93. Tokyo: Kodansha.

———. 1970. *Japanese Society*. Berkeley: University of California Press.

———. 1967. *Tate-shakai no ningen-kankei: Tanitsu-shakai no riron*. Tokyo: Kodansha.

Nitobe, Inazo. 1905. *Bushido: The Soul of Japan*. Reprint, Tokyo: Charles E. Tuttle, 1969.

Pelto, Pertti J. 1968. "The Differences between 'Tight' and 'Loose' Societies." *Transaction*, 37–40.

Reischauer, Edwin O. 1988. *The Japanese Today: Change and Continuity*. Cambridge, MA: Belknap Press.

Shirakashi, Sanshiro. 1985. "Social Loafing of Japanese Students." *Hiroshima Forum for Psychology* 10, 35–40.

Stewart, Edward, and Milton J. Bennett. 1991. *American Cultural Patterns: A Cross-Cultural Perspective*, 2d ed. Yarmouth, ME: Intercultural Press.

Takaki, Ronald. 1989. *Strangers from a Different Shore: A History of Asian Americans*. New York: Penguin Books.

Takano, Yohtaro., and E. Osaka. 1999. "A Supported Common View: Comparing Japan and the U.S. on Individualism/Collectivism." *Asian Journal of Social Psychology* 2, no. 3, 311–41.

———. 1997. "Nihonjin no shuudanshugi to Amerikajin no kojinshugi: Tsuusetsu no saikentou." *Japanese Journal of Psychology* 68, 312–27.

Takeuchi, Musayuki, Hidenaka Wakayama, Ryuji Okada, and David Matsumoto. 2001. "Intercultural Adjustment Potential in Japanese Judo Players." Paper presented at the 2001 Annual Conference of the Japanese Association for Physical Eduation, Sapporo, Japan.

Triandis, Harry C. 1995. *New Directions in Social Psychology: Individualism and Collectivism*. Boulder, CO: Westview Press.

———. 1994. *Culture and Social Behavior*. New York: McGraw-Hill.

Triandis, Harry C., R. Bontempo, M. J. Villareal, M. Hsai, et al. 1988. "Individualism and Collectivism: Cross-Cultural Perspectives on Self-Ingroup Relationships," *Journal of Personality and Social Psychology* 54, no. 2, 323–38.

Yamagishi, Toshio. 1988a. "Exit from the Group as an Individualistic Solution to the Free Rider Problem in the United States and Japan." *Journal of Experimental Social Psychology* 24, 530–42.

———. 1988b. "The Provision of a Sanctioning System in the United States and Japan." *Social Psychology Quarterly* 51, 265–71.

Yamaguchi, Susumu, D. M. Kuhlman, and S. Sugimori. 1995. "Personality Correlates of Allocentric Tendencies in Individualist and Collectivistic Cultures." *Journal of Cross-Cultural Psychology* 26, 658–72.

Yamaguchi, Susumu, Koichi Okamoto, and Takashi Oka. 1985. "Effects of Coactors' Presence: Social Loafing and Social Facilitation." *Japanese Psychological Research* 27, 215–22.

Yamamoto, Tsunetomo. 1979. *Hagakure: The Book of the Samurai*. Tokyo: Kodansha.

Index

A

absentee fathers, 118–21, 171–72
All Japan Judo Federation, 192, 194
Asahi Shimbun (newspaper) surveys:
    1996: 69, 70, 71, 77, 81
    1997: 21, 24, 81
    1998: 21–22, 23, 125, 200
athletes, Japanese:
    emerging reality of, 162
    traditional, 161–62
athletes, professional
    as role models, 158, 159–61

B

Benedict, Ruth, 7, 111
"Big Bang," 22
Buddhism, 18, 42
bullying:
    nontolerance of, 173–74
    as problem in schools, 150–51
    and changing cultural and moral values, 127

S